GENERATING YOUR OWN
Happiness

IT'S TIME FOR PURPOSE,
PASSION, AND POWER

CINNAMON
ALVAREZ

the
publishing
CIRCLE

THE PUBLISHING CIRCLE
Regarding: Cinnamon Alvarez
Suite 310
Cheyenne, Wyoming 82001

GENERATING YOUR OWN HAPPINESS / CINNAMON ALVAREZ
First Edition
ISBN 978-1-947398-05-4

COVER & BOOK INTERIOR DESIGN BY MICHELE UPLINGER

DEDICATION

*I give my love and appreciation
to all the amazing women (and the few men)
who participated in my Jazzercise classes
over the span of fifteen remarkable years.
It's clear that my role wasn't as much instructor
as it was student.
You were each an amazing gift,
providing an opportunity for me
to allow my light to shine
and for my soul to expand.
I fell in love with each
and every one of you.*

TABLE OF CONTENTS

FOREWORD

THE WORLD SEEMS MORE chaotic today than in our past. We are living at a speed and pace never experienced before in history. We have issues and challenges ahead like nothing ever experienced on this planet. While we enjoy more opportunities and options than our ancestors, we also experience accompanying levels of stress that are far higher than any other generation has known.

The world and how we live are being reinvented, making modern life confusing—especially if you don't know exactly what you want. It can be frightening when all the constructs you have lived by are disappearing right before your eyes.

Yes, we are living in stressful but interesting times. However, we each have the ability to craft our own life. We have the tools and technology to generate the destiny we want for ourselves. We have the ability to generate, from the ground up, our own _____ (fill in the blank). Never before have we had so much power to support ourselves and generate the life of our choosing. Surely happiness awaits us all in this new frontier of human life.

But, despite our choices, people are not happy right now and don't know where the key to happiness lies. There is despair and fear in the air because things don't look like they have in the past. We need to look forward using fresh eyes, a perspective you need for genuine happiness and one this book may provide.

It is only when we understand how we work and operate in the world that we can explore all our options. Happiness is not simply an emotion; it's something you become. It is a skill set that will provide you with an edge to generate more of whatever you want.

People and opportunities are drawn to authentic happiness. Happy people sell more and have more clients and opportunities. Their colleagues and acquaintances find them interesting. If your happiness is authentic and real, you will have deeper relationships and enjoy life more fully.

And because we have more opportunities now than ever, happiness, as a skill is more valuable. Luckily, this book outlines the happiness skill set one must learn to have a rich and fulfilling life. Happiness, you will see, is the foundation on which we can build our dreams.

When we are truly happy and know how to generate happiness, we are never out of opportunities, friends, or adventures. The power to generate your own _____ (whatever you want) is the new way to live, a process that is gaining traction and growing around the world.

Whatever you want in this world, you can generate for yourself. For example, people are currently generating their own lifestyles, income, opportunities, and wealth. We are at a pivotal time in history where technological advances provide us with an endless variety of opportunities for happiness and freedom, and jobs are trending to a gig-economy style.

It may appear a bit "woo woo" to you, but if you've picked up this book, you're ready to discover how to identify what's most important to you. So, honor your greatness within and learn how to let go of old, limiting beliefs. Build a rocking, rich life and generate your own happiness.

In this book are the keys to *your* kingdom. You will find answers to generating the happiness you desire. But here is my warning: happiness is a skill set, not an instant manifestation. It is the skill set of knowing and understanding *you*. It is the ability to meet yourself in a new and different way.

If you answer the questions provided here and dig deep, you will unearth your innate happiness. If you are not willing to do that, put this book back on the shelf. Don't waste your time and money if you aren't ready to generate real happiness. Continue living your false happiness and wait until you want to get real.

But if you are ready to get real, let's not waste another moment. Let's get started now. May the wind be at your back!

VICKIE HELM
BEST-SELLING AUTHOR OF *ULTIMATE FREEDOM:*
UNLOCK THE SECRETS TO A LIFE OF PASSION,
PURPOSE, AND PROSPERITY

PREFACE

THANK YOU IN ADVANCE for reading the pages that follow. My wish is that you not only gain valuable insight but that you discover or rediscover something near and dear to your heart and take on seeing it through to fruition.

This work is a result of my honoring a deep knowing that this was what was next for me. I didn't know how to write a book. I just had the experience of knowing. It took something to see it through. It took perseverance, ongoing support, and trust that there was a message of value.

The content and suggested approaches are a compilation from years of study, research and personal experience. That being said, there is a notable difference between knowing or understanding something and applying it to your own life, so I have included exercises at the end of each chapter. However, I chose to use the words, "Let's Play." Sometimes we get a little too serious, so I hope to make this light. I encourage you to engage with the material—to try it on for yourself and give it your all. You have nothing to lose.

With love and appreciation for who you are and what's important to you, let's go!

CINNAMON ALVAREZ

INTRODUCTION

THROUGHOUT LIFE, PEOPLE WHO care about us have said, "I just want you to be happy." And if asked what we want for our children and those we care about most, our answer is usually the same. Apparently, we assume that if you are happy, your life must be good.

I believe in the sincerity of these heartfelt wishes for happiness, but many live deeply unhappy lives and lack satisfaction. In fact, more people live unhappy lives than happy ones.

Like most young adults, I wanted to find happiness, wealth, and success. I don't know about you, but many of us, including myself, were taught that happiness was something you pursued. So, of course, I went searching.

It is even a promise in the Declaration of Independence that we have the right to "pursue happiness." This historical document gave many of us a sense that we needed to chase after and find happiness. Happiness was somewhere out there, and it seemed to be something worth searching for.

We all set off to pursue happiness and attain that ever-elusive "enough," and this is where things fall apart. The confusion is in working to *become enough*, meaning, if you just look hard enough, work diligently enough, do well enough, and are good enough, then you will somehow be happy. If you are respectful to bosses and co-workers, if you are a good spouse, parent, or mother, then eventually you will have the happiness and the respect you deserve in your life. Right? You will find the perfect soul-mate and create a loving family and have the career, success, and wealth you want.

Why? Because you will finally be good enough to have it. And part of being good, we all learned, is to live a life of kindness to others, but that sometimes becomes an "unhealthy kindness" that leads to self-sacrifice.

Thus we focus on others and their wishes, hoping this will lead to happiness. We yearn to make a difference in the world, yet we often discount or neglect our own interests, wishes and, sometimes, even well-being by putting the needs of others above our own. Can you see how this creates unhappiness? This is the great lie many have bought and could be why so many are unhappy, depressed, and frustrated with life.

In this book, we will tear apart the lies we've been sold, told, and controlled by for years. My hope is that you'll come to understand how we fall into the unhappiness trap and then learn how to generate your own happiness. You will discover how to break through deceptions. That means you can finally stop searching for happiness and start enjoying life.

If you want to be authentically happy, deepen your relationships, lower your stress, and have more success in every area of life, you will find those secrets in this book. But here is my warning: happiness is not something you find; it is something you become by letting your greatness shine. This means you have to know yourself, love yourself, and act in accordance with that which speaks to your heart and soul to operate at maximum happiness.

If you are willing to get in touch with your soul and know yourself completely, then you are ready to become happy. If you are not, you will continue your search for happiness. You can either do what you have always done or take the incredibly powerful, bold step by reading this book and engaging in the process of generating your own happiness.

Here's to your happiness and the power to generate anything your heart desires with purpose and passion!

GENERATING YOUR OWN

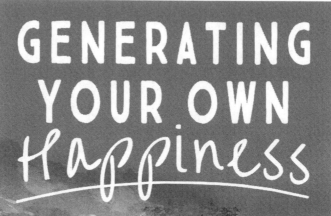

Happiness

IT'S TIME
FOR
PURPOSE,
PASSION,
AND
POWER

CINNAMON ALVAREZ

Foreword by VICKIE HELM
Best-selling author of Ultimate Freedom: Unlock the Secrets
to a Life of Passion, Purpose and Prosperity

CHAPTER 1

HAPPINESS

IN OUR DAY-TO-DAY interactions with others, most people report everything is "fine." People try to put on a happy face, but probably aren't singing lyrics from their favorite song as they go about their typical day. Do you ever people watch? It's apparent that for most, "feeling fine" doesn't equate with a high-quality, superb, wonderful, exquisite, or first-rate life. Instead, "I'm fine," has become one of the most routine lies people tell.

As a society, we have more or less changed the meaning of the word "fine" to mean acceptable or satisfactory, rather than meaning exceptionally good. Many people are not happy, despite what they say. Most would report being unsatisfied in at least one major area of life, and we all have concerns about the future.

The thing about the canned response, "I'm fine," is that most people are not even aware of their current state of "*not* fine." Imagine if, instead, your response to "How are you?" was not only genuine but specific. What if you reported your current state with a heightened awareness of your position in relation to the rest of the world?

People are generally trapped in negativity, or they have numbed themselves to it. In contrast, I want you to be able to authentically describe your current state as "superb, optimistic, concerned, motivated, and up to something big." If and when you are faced with catastrophic events, my wish is that you have the energy behind R.E.M.'s hit song *It's the End of the World as We Know It (And I Feel Fine)*. Sure enough, you will experience challenges throughout the rest of your life, but will you face every event with optimism and vitality?

Our ancestors could have barely imagined the twenty-first century. Life expectancy continues to increase as technology grows exponentially. True, there is growing concern about the world economy and terrorism, and we face a humanitarian crisis as we ponder the scarcity of our resources and the instability of many governments. At the same time, there has been a growing global interest in using happiness and subjective well-being as primary indicators of the quality of human development. Why?

Leading experts worldwide—across the fields of economics, psychology, survey analysis, national statistics, health, public policy, and more—measure happiness and describe how measurements of well-being can be used effectively to assess the progress of nations. Many governments, communities, and organizations are using happiness data and the results of subjective well-being research to develop and enable policies. That's right, happiness.

The World Happiness Report focuses on the complex nuances of happiness data collected from people in over 150 countries. The editors make the argument that happiness is a better indicator of human welfare than measuring variables like real GDP per capita, healthy life expectancy, etc. separately. For example, healthy people are overall happier, but as the reports demonstrate, happier people are overall healthier.

You may be surprised that the data collected for the 2017 World Happiness Report indicates that happiness in the United States is declining due to social rather than economic causes. How often do you focus on improving your finances or stress about your health yet underestimate the importance of your happiness?

Studies from the field of Positive Psychology show that happy people have a competitive advantage over unhappy people: they live longer, are healthier, are more creative, are more intelligent, and make more money. Happy people are more likely to be in leadership roles; they are better liked . . . I could go on and on. Yet, as Gallup reports, the vast majority worldwide "are emotionally disconnected" and are less likely to be productive. As Nancy Etcoff, an evolutionary psychologist at Harvard says, "Well-being should be developed both for its own sake and for its side effects."

It's interesting to me that most of the clients I have worked with, and really most people in general, think they are already happy. If you were to take a survey of the people in your immediate circles, asking them to rate how happy they are on a scale of one to ten, most people would rank themselves pretty high, probably between seven and nine.

However, in my decades of studying personal transformation, and working with people to help them generate their own happiness, I have observed confusion. This misunderstanding keeps us from being authentically happy. It keeps people from knowing how, or even learning how, they can generate their own happiness. What I have found is that most people confuse being safe and comfortable with being happy.

It's not your fault. Our primal instinct is to survive. We learn to seek safety and security—in addition to love, acceptance, and significance. It's believed that these primal instincts are engrained in us because of our dependence while we're young. Compared to other offspring, rabbits for example, can go it alone in the wild within three weeks of age. Humans rely on maternal nurture while we develop into complex cultural beings. Human infants are especially helpless because, to fit through the birth canal, the brain at the time of birth is less than thirty percent of the size of the adult brain. In fact, the prefrontal cortex in humans is not fully developed until we're about twenty-three years old. Much of our development and learning is done within the culture in which we live.

Somehow people have learned to equate happiness with long-term security, comfort, and safety. We seek it out. Perhaps it's because of a deep-rooted fear of abandonment or uncertainty. Yet, generating your own happiness is really one of the biggest, riskiest, and scariest experiences a person can go through because it takes you out of your comfort zone. It's much easier to have comfort and safety than it is to create what you truly want or to tap into the pursuits that will make you genuinely happy.

Over time, confusing happiness with safety and comfort leads to depression, anxiety, a lack of growth, boredom, resentment, and a loss of quality of life. You enjoy fewer successes when you don't understand true happiness and know how to generate it. Wouldn't you agree that real, true success in life includes an authentic experience of happiness?

People who suffer and hide from deep pain, unable to generate their own happiness, have instead learned the habit of indulging. They indulge in pleasures that create a pseudo feeling of happiness. They get confused, thinking that indulging in feel-good activities will make them happy.

When we do this, what are we avoiding? We are avoiding feelings of unhappiness. We secretly think pursuing pleasure and comfort will create happiness. Instead, we create, at best, temporary diversion. And, thanks to the cunning skills of marketers, many are addicted to pleasure, comfort, and safety, having no real idea of how to generate their own happiness.

I hope you are asking yourself, *Am I one of those people who secretly believes that generating my own happiness is seeking comfort, pleasure, and safety?* I'm going to be bold and assert it is plausible—highly likely, actually—that you are one of those people. You may not realize it because you are lying to yourself, but most people aren't really that happy at all. They may feel satisfied because they've settled, but they aren't actually happy. And there's a big difference in outcome between settling and experiencing happiness.

So, let me ask you: are you up for the challenge of truly looking at your life and finding out how to generate your own happiness? If you are, it will change you, but bear in mind that generating your own happiness isn't easy or convenient. It takes something. It takes a willingness to look within and let go of old notions.

⁓

We're going to look at the life of a woman we'll call Sally. Quickly we will see that happiness isn't the result of acquiring shiny possessions, pleasing others, or climbing the ladder of success—although the media and modern society lead us to assume it is.

I want us to examine the potential problems that result in pursuing the wealth and status we now see as necessary to our happiness. Do we actually seek the shiny and new to escape our lives? People feel like they can't be happy when things aren't picture perfect, when things don't go as planned. The same is true when things are unfamiliar. Why? Because people have confused happiness with things being flawless, easy, and familiar.

The truth is that happiness is a skill set in which the foundational skill is the ability to challenge who you think you are, in each moment, and produce a different outcome. Unfortunately, we're taught happiness is conforming to a set of rules or societal norms, and that's where people get confused. This is not happiness. It's submission; it's resignation. Living in this manner does not require dreams or goals; it does not require knowing your thoughts or wishes. It simply requires that you get on board with whatever agenda is present.

Being happy doesn't mean you always look happy. It doesn't mean you wake up, jumping out of bed saying, "Woohoo!" What inner happiness does is allow you to challenge your status quo and manage your inner state of being. It's the ability to tame your mind when your mind has run amuck with negative, toxic thinking. It's an option you choose to engage with that generates opportunities, healthy relationships, and other advantages. It doesn't mean you don't go through difficult periods. It doesn't mean you avoid sickness, death, or hard times. It does mean your mind is open to options, possibilities, and a healthy perspective—things an unhappy mind is not open to.

Unhappiness doesn't allow for possibilities or opportunities, because it's closed-minded. It's a breeding ground for deeper problems, like depression and self-loathing. Unhappiness *believes* it is doomed to a life of unhappiness because it only focuses on what is not ideal or comfortable.

On the other hand, knowing how to generate your own happiness gives you the tools to move through hard times and the ability to use those hard times, to learn from them and grow through them without creating more resentment or anger. If you cannot generate your own happiness, you will eventually find yourself struggling and stuck in life.

It's important, however, to understand the difference between generating your own happiness and being in a constant state of pleasure. Most people mistakenly believe that having constant pleasure—things being easy, always getting your way, and preventing unfortunate events—is the definition of happiness. As long as they avoid pain and suffering, most people think they're happy. They confuse being happy with getting their way all the time. This is not happiness, it's self-indulgence.

Happiness is a state of mind and an attitude of the heart. It is being in command of yourself and your destiny. It is a discipline and a practice that requires you to know what you want, what your values are, and what you would like to experience in your life. In short, it requires you to know yourself. Happiness is the state of honoring yourself and being true to what you want; it's knowing and respecting your values, skill sets, and desires.

Earlier, we considered the "pursuit of happiness" as stated in the Declaration of Independence. It is something to pursue, but you must follow the right target. Happiness is when you pursue your chosen values and accept some degree of risk to grow the life you envision. It is the great adventure of building your desires and dreams. It is the practice of growing, trusting, and honoring who you are.

The process of generating happiness is what you will learn in the chapters that follow. We will discover how people give away their happiness and don't even realize it. We will explore how this happens and what you can do to avoid it. Remember, being happy is an ability, something you can learn. It's having the know-how to claim and live life according to your dreams.

This is a valuable skill because, from an early age, we are taught to live according to someone else's rules, wishes, values, and commands. We don't often explore what it is that we want. Instead, we are praised for helping others, following the rules, being a good team player, and thinking of others above ourselves.

These societal norms are the very rules that have sabotaged our happiness and allowed us to become numb to what we actually want out of life. We pursue careers in which corporations exploit us and ask us to think about company growth over our own dreams. As a result, many people reach a level of success professionally but are unhappy because they have lost their sense of self. They have an exceptional set of honed corporate skills, but don't know who they are.

These top performers know how to lean in, follow directions, work late, and overachieve. Yet, they often wonder why they get burned out, taken for granted, and overworked—never once considering what it is they really want. They become discouraged by constant demands, yet they do not see how they have brought these demands on themselves with the choices they've made.

In the following chapters, as we follow Sally's journey, you will see firsthand how she's become lost and discouraged. We will consider how people are manipulated out of their happiness and what they can do to regain control. You will discover why happiness is such a powerful tool and how to use it to give you more success, stronger relationships, and healthier boundaries.

The power to generate your own happiness begins with understanding how we disempower ourselves and become unhappy. Therefore, we will first observe how Sally has become trapped and disillusioned. Then we will discover how she regains and empowers her happiness—and how you can, too. I invite you to journey with Sally in her pursuit of happiness. Happiness always begins with meeting yourself.

LET'S PLAY:

- **ANSWER THESE QUESTIONS:**

- **IN THE PAST, HOW HAVE YOU DEFINED HAPPINESS?**

- **WHAT DOES THE PURSUIT OF HAPPINESS LOOK LIKE FOR YOU?**

- **HAVE YOU PUT OFF OWNING AND EXAMINING YOUR OWN UNHAPPINESS? IF SO, WHY?**

CHAPTER 2

MEET SALLY DO-IT-ALL

SHE LIFTED HER HANDS from the keyboard, leaned back into her chair, looked out her window into the setting sun, and caught a glimpse of her solemn reflection in the glass. The rest of the building was nearly silent because everyone else had gone home. Another week had passed, and there she was, still working, feeling exhausted and discouraged by all that remained undone. Overworked and underappreciated, Sally was expected to finish it all.

Like all successful women, Sally had worked hard to get to the top, but it came with more than her share of responsibilities. She was the go-to gal for pretty much any problem, be it work or family related. Working late into the night and putting off doing anything for herself was common.

Just the idea of taking time off for a holiday or a vacation added to her stress because she knew there would be a pile of work on her desk, waiting for her return. Nothing seemed to happen unless she was in her office, working all the time.

To her peers, she had made it. Outwardly, it looked as if Sally had everything. She had respect from top clients and colleagues. She was her own boss, called the shots, and set her own (long) hours. Heck, she thought she had made it too. She certainly had come a long way.

Yet she felt stuck in the rat race. She pushed herself through the day and still ran out of time, with her to-do-list left unfinished. Although Sally made over six figures and often treated herself to luxuries, material things hardly seemed to matter now. She was so tired, all she could feel was a desire to shut down mentally and physically.

More and more, she found herself getting irritated, feeling overwhelmed, and lacking motivation. She found herself setting goals but rarely achieving them because she was too busy helping others achieve their goals. Sally just couldn't understand why she wasn't happy and questioned what had happened to her go-get-'em enthusiasm and love for life.

She wondered, *Why is this happening? Why am I not motivated and happy? I have a stable job. I'm in a leadership position. I make more money than the average woman. What's wrong with me? I don't have any help or support. I have no freedom. I'm tired. I just want to feel inspired again.* Then she felt ashamed to be complaining because she thought she had no right to be upset. After all, she had been so fortunate.

Instead, she tried focusing on things she was grateful for since she learned of the many benefits of gratitude at the yearly women's business conference she attended. She quietly began thanking the universe for everything she had. Although she was sincerely appreciative for what she did have, she could not fight that deep-down feeling that there had to be more. A loud, internal voice rang through her mind: *I want more . . . more freedom, more love, more money, more support, more connection . . . I want to reach my full potential.*

Sally felt guilty for wanting more, but she was tired of feeling stagnant and stuck. She couldn't seem to get ahead. She wanted to be happy and yearned to get more out of life but didn't know how to achieve that.

Can you relate to Sally's dilemma?

Are you, like Sally, sick and tired of being stuck in the rat race, running out of time every day with things undone? Do you often feel so tired and defeated that you could collapse, cry, or, worse, rip someone's head off because you've been stuffing emotions? Do you have high hopes and aspirations, but they seem unachievable? Or have you been so discouraged you've lost sight of your dreams altogether?

How often do you have inspiration-crushing experiences? How often are you frustrated, distracted, or irritated by something over which you have no control? Do you find yourself feeling totally overwhelmed, not knowing where to start, what to do, or how to change your current circumstances?

Do you find yourself giving up on doing things for yourself because they seem unrealistic or you have no time for them? Do you feel as if you have to do everything yourself because there is no one you can count on? Or do you ever find yourself thinking, *I don't have enough time, money, support, or experience to achieve this goal*?

All that being said, are you proud of yourself for how hard you've worked for everything you have? Have you overcome significant obstacles? Do you know, deep down, that you're capable of more (if you just had the support you need)? Do you have a vision for something big, but don't know how to get there? Do you lack confidence in your capabilities? Are you discouraged or second guessing yourself? If so, know that it is okay to want more out of life—even if you don't yet see how to achieve it.

Year after year, misguided resolutions are made by those who think success will make them happy. A lot of people set out to accomplish something because they have a fervent desire or think they should change something about themselves or their life, but the majority of people aren't successful.

Losing weight is a great example. People are usually more motivated by their image than their health. The desire to lose weight stems from being unhappy about their current body image; it's a desire to fix something believed to be bad or wrong. Going to the gym and/or stepping on a scale is a reminder that they aren't happy with themselves as they are. Their focus is negative, yet they wonder why they aren't motivated to work out more often.

Many people avoid setting goals outside their comfort level and resist making promises altogether because they don't want to fail or be deemed as someone who is "all talk" if they think there is a chance that what they want may be unachievable. They have a picture of what it means to fail, as if not hitting their target means *they* are a failure. Many people will do almost anything in an attempt not to look bad or be judged—even when they are their own worst critic. Others simply like to play it safe to avoid the discomfort of the unknown—even if it means staying unsatisfied with the same old situation.

Most people are looking for a magical solution to their troubles, hoping that when they find it, they will finally be happy. They equate success as happiness, yet both keep eluding them, and they don't know why. But remember, people who are happy have taught themselves how to become happy. Your ability to generate happiness is something you grow into, in the same way you develop any new skill.

For example, children do not drive cars. We all accept one must grow into that ability. Instead, we start with crawling, then walking, then riding a tricycle, skateboard, and bicycle. Finally, we learn to drive. Happiness, like driving, is not what we are taught in the early stages of life. Instead, we learn unhealthy forms of thinking, speaking, and boundary keeping, along with the unhealthy habit of ignoring our callings, feelings, and dreams. With loving intention, we are told to be nice, fit in, and be a team player. This is actually the beginning of unhappiness, yet it has been going on for generations, all over the world.

Most people don't know how to become happy because they have never been taught. I, too, had to learn how to generate my own happiness, and I began with baby steps, just like you will. When you finish this book, you will know how to drive the vehicle of you and *become* the happiness you desire.

In order for this to happen, we must look at how we get caught up in doing-it-all for others, hoping that, after it is all done, we will find happiness. This lie keeps you seeking happiness without ever becoming truly happy. It's time to stop being a Sally Do-It-All and start being happy. Do you realize how much you do in a day?

Most successful professionals and small business owners do the job of three or four people in a day. Then they go home to their families and, again, do-it-all. At the end of the evening, they fall over because they are exhausted. Is this you? It's time to understand that nothing will make you unhappier than running yourself ragged.

LET'S PLAY:

- GO TO WWW.GENERATINGYOUROWNHAPPINESS.COM AND DOWNLOAD THE WORKSHEET "DO-IT-ALL TIME EVALUATION" AND LET'S SEE WHAT TAKES PRIORITY IN YOUR LIFE.

- HOW MUCH "DOING-IT-ALL" DO YOU DO? IDENTIFY THE AREAS IN WHICH YOU FEEL OVERWHELMED.

CHAPTER 3

YOUR DREAM OR
THE AMERICAN DREAM?

SALLY, LIKE MOST OF US, grew up pursuing the clichés she was given by parents and teachers: "You can do anything you put your mind to"; "Work hard and you'll succeed." We've heard these encouraging lines time and time again from well-meaning authority figures, right? And, if we looked around us, the classmates, friends, and coworkers who were living by the mantra of study hard, get into a good college, and get a good job were being rewarded, right?

Somehow the standard clichés about hard work, success, and happiness are supposed to comfort us, to reassure us we are on the right path. We believe if we simply follow the advice that's been passed down through generations, we will have a happy life. So we try to follow society's rules to achieve happiness. We start believing that happiness is a set of instructions, not a personal choice. Every day, billions of people evaluate whether they should be happy or not by other people's standards of success, instead of their own.

Trillions of dollars are spent every year in pursuing happiness via the ever-elusive American Dream. We throw money at dieting, medications, cosmetic surgery, fashion, or the latest and greatest technology. We chase wealth and the status and power that comes with it. Still, people aren't really that happy.

The average American thinks happiness is something he can buy. Just look at the definition of happiness being marketed to us. Where do we spend our time and money? If we're really honest, most people want to be something like the images we see online, on TV, and in movies and magazines. But why? Why do we think the media's portrayal of happiness is true?

We believe the clichés and follow the ads because we equate pleasure and success with happiness. We don't typically want to think of ourselves as striving to keep up with the Joneses; we don't want to be seen as shallow or to admit we are focused on status and appearance, yet we strive to have x, be y, and achieve z because we think it will make us happy. And, like it or not, this is what we've been taught to do.

We believe that to be happy, we must first _____ (fill in the blank). We start fishing for happiness by making ourselves look like the most attractive bait. We acquire symbols of success, seek the recognition of others, and buy more cool stuff. It's like we are fishing and using ourselves for the bait. We throw that bait into the world and hope we find something or someone who will make us happy. Then, we are completely beside ourselves when no one takes the bait.

We set ourselves up for disappointment, not only because our goals are inauthentic and unrealistic, but also because we're focusing on what we don't have and what we don't like about our lives. We think we'll be happy if and when we get the promotion, find our soulmate, and are the perfect image of youth and vitality. We make it all about external acquisition.

We get stuck going through the motions, pursuing our perception of what happiness looks like, not realizing we've bought the lies marketed to us. I, too, have fallen into the trap of pursuing more happiness. Achieving a sense of accomplishment is satisfying: *Yes! I've been successful.* You may even think, *I've been blessed. I've accomplished what people have said couldn't be done. I've built profitable businesses. I fit into the size four jeans and can ski the double black diamond runs. I found and married the love of my life, and we live the American Dream in the land of opportunity.*

However, when I live authentically, lit up and inspired by true happiness, I find myself being asked, "What's your secret?" Upon reflecting on my happiest and most rewarding moments, I can see that most, if not all, include an authentic, conscious willingness to be on what I best describe as the roller-coaster of life. Happiness means creating, connecting with, and appreciating people, and feeling like I'm making a difference (or at least yearning to).

My most satisfying accomplishments all started with the voice in my head saying, *I can do that,* coupled with feeling inspired or having a sense of knowing or a calling. Happiness doesn't come with possessions or a prescribed path to success. It is simply the ability to listen to your heart and follow that calling within you.

My fondest memories include sharing my beautiful self with other beautiful souls and having sincere gratitude. These memories range from shedding a tear of appreciation and admiration for the amazing people in my life to having the experience of being one with nature. Just reminiscing evokes the rich yet serene emotion of that happiness.

That doesn't mean everything always goes my way. I've made plenty of mistakes. I've experienced my share of struggles and hurts. I still experience frustration, discouragement, and disappointment. I still cry. I've been confronted by my limiting beliefs and negative thoughts, such as *I'm not good enough; I don't know how; nobody cares;* and *I have to do it all by myself.* In fact, it was almost as though I was being tested while writing this book, even though I thought I had transformed most of my limiting beliefs long ago.

Negative thoughts are where most people get trapped and give up. They tend to throw in the towel and turn to mind-numbing comforts (like eating)—myself included. But, do you know how to recognize your own limiting beliefs? Do you know when to push through self-sabotage and unforeseen obstacles? How do you know when to surrender?

Sally finds herself rundown, increasingly depleted by the job she thought would fulfill her. She's been on the prescribed path to success for so long she thinks she should feel more buoyant. Like Sally, many people live on auto-pilot, letting life just happen to them, repeating habitual patterns and succumbing to emotional responses. When life happens, they get stopped in their tracks, unable to move past their old habits. For them, it appears as if something out of their control has happened, and the feeling of being out of control creates powerlessness and unhappiness.

Sally is beginning to awaken to the need for change. You may have also said to yourself, *Something needs to change if I'm going to feel happy.* It's true that something does need to change, but the circumstances beyond our control are not the problem. Instead, how you think needs to change. To generate your own happiness, you must be willing to ask yourself, *What have I told myself, time and time again, that works* for me *or* against me?

Creating more happiness means knowing yourself and becoming more aware of how you operate. Are you willing to accept guidance from within, rather than give away your power by following the societal norm? We give away our power by looking outside ourselves for instructions or solutions, instead of listening to and trusting our inner guidance.

If you're not happy with your life and often feel you need to do something different, or if you feel like something is missing, you're not alone.

Ask yourself, *What do I want most out of life?* Previously when asking myself this question, most of my answers had something to do with health, wealth, love, and making a difference. Now when I ask myself what I want most, I know I want to honor what my soul wants. I trust that in doing so, it will be for the greatest and highest good (including myself as part of the greater whole).

This means you must beware of what I call the "in-order-to" mindset, which is the idea that you need something "out there" to change in order to be happy. Until you let go of the idea that happiness comes as a result of accomplishments, things you acquire, or somewhere you get to, you will never be genuinely happy.

You must understand that the process of engaging with your inner calling is what generates the greatest sense of fulfillment. Happiness is in loving and appreciating "what is" in your life—all of it!

LET'S PLAY:

START TO IDENTIFY WHAT MAKES YOU HAPPY. REFLECT UPON YOUR HAPPIEST AND MOST REWARDING MOMENTS:

- WHAT LIGHTS YOU UP?

- WHAT HAS TRIGGERED YOU TO TAKE ACTION IN AN AREA THAT HAS PROVEN TO BE REWARDING?

- WHAT HAVE YOU TOLD YOURSELF THAT WORKS FOR YOU?

- WHAT DO YOU TELL YOURSELF, TIME AND TIME AGAIN, THAT WORKS AGAINST YOU?

- WHAT COULD YOU SAY INSTEAD?

CHAPTER 4

⌒〜⌒

SALLY MELTS DOWN
FROM "SHOULDING"

IT WAS SALLY'S BIRTHDAY. Although her girlfriends took her out to lunch and everyone at the office wished her a happy birthday, she did not feel happy. Instead, she sat there reflecting on how another year had flown by with nothing really to show for it.

She wasn't where she wanted to be at this stage in her life; she had pictured her life differently. Sure, she had a high-paying job; sure, she looked successful; and sure, her friends thought she was successful, too. But the truth was, she felt like she expended a lot of energy for nothing. She couldn't seem to get ahead.

She thought to herself, *All this work and so little to show for it. I should be debt free and have more money saved up by now. I should have more free time.*

I shouldn't get stressed out. I should be more appreciative of the fact that I have a job. I should have an amazing, loving relationship with someone I can count on. Is this all I have to look forward to, working day in and day out, chasing the clock and putting out fires? There's always something more I have to pay for, and I never have time to do anything for myself. I can't ever get ahead. Why does the entire burden always fall on me? Most people spend their whole life just chasing after what I have, but I have it, and I am still not happy. Who am I to complain? I chose this life and did it to myself. What's wrong with me?

Sally had barely managed to meet her big deadline, but thanks to a pep talk with her friend the day before and her sense of responsibility, she got it done. She should have felt relieved because she had finished her project on time, but she was so exhausted. All she really wanted was to go home, drink a glass of wine, and sleep. Sally wanted relief from the dissatisfaction and depression slowly creeping into her life.

She could feel her body wanting to shut down, both mentally and physically. The last thing she wanted to do was go out to dinner with her boyfriend to celebrate her birthday. She felt disconnected from Brian lately. She was unsure about moving forward, but she couldn't bear the thoughts of letting him down by confronting him with the truth about her feelings.

She lifted her head and smiled as a sales rep peeked his head in to wish her a happy birthday, but inside she was saying to herself, *I don't know how much longer I can go on like this.*

No one could see Sally's depression, exhaustion, and pain. She hid her secret dissatisfaction from everyone. No one knew the truth about how Sally felt inside. Even Sally spent the day dismissing her feelings and rejecting the notion that anything was wrong with the type of success she had built for herself.

She glanced down at the time on her screen and suddenly remembered that she was supposed to pick up her son early. She felt instant panic and knew there was no possible way she could get there on time, even if she just ran out, leaving everything on her desk unhandled.

She was quietly fighting back the tears. She felt powerless. Too many people were depending on her to continue being the Sally they knew and relied on. Sally felt too responsible to everyone and everything around her even to think about how she could make a better life for herself.

As Sally got into her car, she lost control and couldn't hold back the sadness any longer. She could feel a tear slowly run down her cheek. It was not a happy birthday. Instead, she was having a meltdown.

Sally eventually made it home and poured herself a glass of wine, but it didn't adequately relax her from the exhausting day. At three in the morning, she found herself tossing and turning as her mind raced. In a just a few short hours, she would have to be up, facing another day of obligations and expectations. She didn't know if she could pull it off.

If this is the kind of thing you are quietly doing to yourself, then you, like Sally, are headed for a meltdown. You cannot generate your own happiness by making sure that everyone else is happy first. This has never worked. Consider how you allow your time to be consumed by others and their agendas—without considering what would invigorate you. Being preoccupied by obligations that do not fulfill you will diminish your happiness.

Sally had turned the idea of being of service into endless sacrifice and soul-stifling obligation. We don't realize when this happens. It sneaks in without our awareness. We want to be helpful and suddenly our helpfulness becomes an overwhelming demand for which we sacrifice our well-being.

Let's again explore Sally's mindset and consider what she is saying to herself:

- "I can't ever get ahead, and I don't know how much longer I can live like this."
- "I'm always chasing the clock and putting out fires."
- "Who am I to complain? I chose this life and did it to myself. What's wrong with me?"

This is not what Sally thought was supposed to happen. Doing more and acquiring more has not opened the magical and infinite pool of peace and happiness. And now, not only is she buried under obligation, she's totally discouraged and starting to become depressed.

Let's look at how Sally "shoulds" on herself. Sally has expectations and beliefs for herself about how things should and shouldn't be. She thinks having certain possessions and accomplishing certain things will make her happy. She judges everything by right or wrong, good or bad. She thinks fixing things that are wrong will make life better and make her a better person, not realizing she has placed unrealistic expectations on herself.

For example, Sally thinks she should be able to manage her schedule so she's not stressed all of the time. She thinks she should be more appreciative and less frustrated. She should be noticed and acknowledged for all her hard work—but *shoulding* has never made anyone happy.

And that's not all of it. Sally knows when it's appropriate to bite her tongue, but if you could read her mind, you would discover she's constantly thinking about what she wants to change: *Employees should be able to pull their own weight and meet their deadlines without making a bunch of mistakes. My client shouldn't be such a jerk, always trying to get one over on me. My siblings shouldn't take advantage of me. Men shouldn't look at women as sexual objects. Young women shouldn't flaunt their bodies and then complain about being objectified. Kids shouldn't stand on chairs and make loud screeching noises in public places.* Sally loves rules and standards and *shoulds* on others too.

Does this sound familiar? Can you hear all of the negativity? She's not only setting herself up for disappointment, but it can't be fun for people around her either. People with this kind of thinking are usually tough on everyone, not only themselves.

The following are Sally's thoughts about the proper conditions for success and happiness:

- *I should have well over one-hundred-thousand dollars in the bank and no debt.*
- *I should weigh under 125 pounds.*
- *I should have a loyal, loving spouse who supports me.*
- *I should have an exceptionally well-behaved and intelligent child.*
- *I should have a PhD.*
- *I should give to charity and volunteer for a meaningful cause.*

Sally has a lot of "shoulds." Are you starting to dislike Sally or think her expectations are a bit unrealistic? Or do you relate? Can you see how tough Sally is on herself and how she's setting herself up for disappointment?

Can you see the value in ending this vicious cycle? Sally isn't actually doing what would make her happy; she is following a set of beliefs that most likely have nothing to do with what she really wants. Sally's buying into and creating the expectation that things should be other than how they currently are, yet these are painful judgments that will rob her of happiness.

Sally hasn't even stopped to ask if she really wants any of those things. She's so disconnected from her true self that she has no idea what she wants—other than to get out of the painful cycle. Have you experienced this too?

If you are interested in generating your own happiness, then you will benefit from clearly defining what you want—not defaulting to another's ideas about what should or shouldn't happen. You must recognize the unrealistic expectations you put on yourself and how you are working toward unhealthy, unbalanced goals instead of your true goals and desires. You must retrain yourself to look at what it is you desire in life and move away from other people's standards, beliefs, and requests.

Happiness has never been servitude; it is always the pursuit of what *you* want, even if what you want is to make a difference in the lives of others. Happiness is never the result of pursuing and accomplishing what *others* want from you or for you.

LET'S PLAY:

- START NOTICING THE TYPES OF EXPECTATIONS YOU HAVE. DO THESE EXPECTATIONS TRULY RESONATE, OR HAVE YOU ADOPTED THE EXPECTATIONS OF OTHERS?

- PAY ATTENTION TO HOW OFTEN YOU USE THESE WORDS:
  - SHOULD
  - NEED
  - HAVE TO
  - IN ORDER TO
  - IF ONLY

CHAPTER 5

UNCONDITIONAL LOVE

IT SOUNDS SO CLICHÉ, but you can't expect others to see you as you want to be seen and appreciate you for who you are if you can't first completely love and accept yourself. Self-contempt is another reason why most people can't generate true happiness.

We each wear our love or hatred for ourselves on our sleeves for the rest of the world to see and notice, even when it's not obvious to us. Your joy and your disappointment with your life shows on your face, in your body language, and in everything you do, say, and think. All of how you feel about yourself comes out in your interactions with the world. Believe it or not, there is no hiding this.

It's crucial to recognize how cruel we can be to ourselves. If you want to generate your own happiness, you must first understand how you create your unhappiness. Being mindful of your actions and knowing how you operate will empower you to make new choices, allowing you to do something different.

So often, however, we don't realize just how unkind and cruel we are to ourselves because it's habitual and what we've been taught. We've learned that being humble and selfless is an admirable trait. We've learned that to be successful, we've got to be hard on ourselves and hold ourselves to high standards. Starting at a very young age, we've had our mistakes and inappropriate behavior pointed out to us. We've been told how we *should* have behaved.

All this judgment produces shame, and shame does not motivate people or make them happy. When you continuously tell yourself you should be anything other than what you are, you are quietly telling yourself there is something wrong, that you are broken in some way and must be fixed before you can be happy. When you treat yourself this poorly, you will simply feel disappointed and unhappy.

Not only are we disappointed with life's circumstances, but we're left with the underlying feelings of shame, believing we are to blame somehow. Shame and disappointment are painful because they don't give any opportunity for restitution and leave you disempowered. Imagine your mom or dad telling you they are disappointed in you. That hurts. But what if that same message comes from self-talk and you believe it? It's even more harmful. A critical spirit can quietly sabotage your inner genius and creativity.

This means it's time to stop blaming and shaming yourself. But it can be easier said than done, right? Instead of simply telling yourself you should stop, ask yourself what stopping *shoulding* yourself would look like. How about allowing yourself to appreciate who you are? What would it look like to love your true self unconditionally? Here's a hint: it looks like authentic happiness. This is allowing the power of you to come out.

I think there's something magical about "allowing"—even more so when you couple it with *loving*. Allowing, accepting, or granting, whichever term you relate to best, doesn't mean you have to give up what's important to you or endorse things that are plain wrong. It means you learn to "let be," rather than trying to control, change, or judge that which is not yours.

If you are like most people, then I can safely presume you have said some pretty mean and nasty things to yourself and held yourself to standards you would never impose on others. Think of the last time you stood in front of a full-length mirror and scrutinized what you saw before you.

For example, people often wonder why they can't stick to an exercise regime. Most likely, they are telling themselves that they "should" exercise to fix something they don't like about their body or physical condition. It's no wonder that, for most people, exercise doesn't sound appealing, considering that they associate it with what they don't like about themselves. Instead of being motivated by self-love, they are fixated on self-hatred of their stomach, hips, and thighs; their lack of willpower and motivation; you name it. If you fall into this category, every time you set a goal to work out to lose weight, you're telling yourself you shouldn't be the way you are.

With such a negative focus, it is no wonder so little progress toward health is made, and having negative body image is just one small example of how cruel we can be to ourselves. We're taught to hold ourselves to high standards, and, unfortunately, like Sally, we may be *shoulding* all over ourselves without realizing it.

I suggest taking a moment to forgive yourself for any resentment, anger, or blame directed at yourself. Let go of any judgments you have made. For me, the most impactful exercise has been forgiving myself for forgetting that I am a divine being. In fact, it's an ongoing process.

I know you didn't pick up this book to work on forgiveness. However, the practice of forgiving and loving yourself is an integral part of successfully generating your own happiness. If you are not happy with you, then how can you be happy? You may think there's nothing for you to forgive, but, odds are, you've been subject to hardship and unfortunate events, which have impacted how you see yourself.

It is possible—extremely likely, even—that you've been victimized. We've all experienced some form of trauma, hardship, or adversity, though some may seem more tragic than others. However, even if someone or something else is to blame for your trauma, my guess is that you have also blamed yourself. In fact, your self-judgment is most likely the deepest source of any reoccurring pain you experience.

If you've studied human developmental psychology or done any self-improvement work, you have likely discovered that humans analyze past events and are often left with a sense of not being enough. For example, you may find yourself thinking, *I'm not good enough, smart enough, educated enough, connected enough, or worthy enough.* Pick your demon.

Shoulding yourself reinforces these painful, limiting beliefs and drives us further from self-love. Telling ourselves what we should and shouldn't do/be reinforces the idea that we can't be happy unless we can change certain things about ourselves.

You do not need fixing or self-help so much as you need self-love and acceptance. In fact, if I have one grand purpose in life, one lesson to learn or one golden message to share, it would be to love. Love others. Love all things. Most of all, love yourself unconditionally, in the same way you love the ones you hold dearest, be it your child, mom, dad, or pet.

These examples are given in hopes you can relate to the love I am describing: pure, unconditional love, filled with acceptance and appreciation. It is my opinion that peace and healing are possible if we practice loving and appreciating ourselves and each other in this manner. And, sharing your unique gifts—your distinct abilities and talents to express love—will generate genuine happiness and fulfillment.

LET'S PLAY:

- NOTICE WHEN YOU FOCUS ON TRAITS YOU DON'T LIKE ABOUT YOURSELF. EVEN IF IT FEELS SILLY, PRACTICE SELF-LOVE AND FORGIVING YOURSELF FOR ANY SELF-CRITICISM. WHAT "MISTAKES" HAVE YOU NOT FORGIVEN YOURSELF FOR? ASK YOURSELF IF YOU ARE *WILLING* TO FORGIVE, GROW FROM THE EXPERIENCE AND LOVE YOURSELF UNCONDITIONALLY. GIVE YOURSELF PERMISSION TO BE HAPPY.

- PRACTICE RELEASING NEGATIVITY BY AFFIRMING UNCONDITIONAL LOVE. THERE IS A TECHNIQUE CALLED

"TAPPING" THAT WAS ORIGINALLY DISCOVERED BY DR. ROGER CALLAHAN AND THEN LATER IMPROVED UPON BY GARY CRAIG IN WHAT'S CALLED EMOTIONAL FREEDOM TECHNIQUES (EFT). CALLAHAN DISCOVERED THAT BY TAPPING ON THE MERIDIAN POINTS OF THE BODY, PEOPLE STARTED TO FEEL BETTER. CRAIG FOUND THAT BY USING CERTAIN PHRASES TO ACCOMPANY THE TAPPING, HE COULD INCREASE THE POSITIVE EFFECTS. I'VE ADAPTED THAT LANGUAGE AND FIND IT TO BE SUCCESSFUL FOR PRACTICING UNCONDITIONAL LOVE WITHOUT THE USE OF TAPPING. I THINK YOU'LL SEE THE BENEFITS! YOU CAN USE THIS SAMPLE SENTENCE: "EVEN THOUGH I _____ (FILL IN THE BLANK), I COMPLETELY AND UNCONDITIONALLY LOVE, APPRECIATE, AND ACCEPT MYSELF." IF YOU WANT TO LEARN MORE ABOUT TAPPING TECHNIQUES, THERE ARE SEVERAL BOOKS ON THE MARKET.

- ASK YOURSELF WHAT YOU ULTIMATELY WANT. ALLOW YOURSELF TO THINK ABOUT YOUR TRUE WANTS–NOT WHAT YOU THINK YOU SHOULD WANT–AND MAKE ROOM FOR THESE DESIRES TO MANIFEST.

NOTE:

If you find yourself struggling in any capacity, ask for support. Simply talking to someone can give you amazing insight and perspective. If you suspect you're dealing with depression, please seek professional help. This book and the exercises given are in no way meant to treat depression or other health concerns.

CHAPTER 6

⌒

SALLY IS STUCK-IN-A-RUT

SALLY KNOWS SHE IS irreplaceable. Even if the company doesn't know this, she does. Although it feels good to be a valuable asset, she doesn't get a real break, even for vacation, because she doesn't have any support or back up. She realizes it doesn't look like she needs support because she has shown she can do it all.

Well, in the past she could do everything. Now, Sally has lost her drive. She doesn't want anyone to see her struggle, but inside she knows something has changed. Some days it's challenging to get anything accomplished. She used to be efficient and effective. It's like something happened to her "go-get-'em" enthusiasm and determination. She wants her motivation back. How did "Sally Do-It-All" become "Sally Stuck-in-a-Rut?"

Sally now questions whether she has achieved what she wanted in life, but realizes she never asked herself what she wanted. She has, however, asked herself *why* she's not satisfied, and she's been able to come up with many reasons. Her long list of annoyances reinforces her feelings of being stuck. It's not just that Sally can't say no, although that is an issue for her. Sally's problem is she hasn't taken the time to discover what she wants to say yes to.

Everything seems stressful to Sally because she is doing it all. Often, professionals take on more and more and more without setting boundaries or saying no. Because they want the next promotion, or they want to impress others with their work ethic, talents, attitude, and skill. It's easy to become stuck in the rut of taking on more.

In fact, we are taught this habit early on. We are taught to impress by aiming ever higher. We think doing it all, never saying no, is what is required. As a young professional, Sally also set out to prove herself to her family and the world. She had lofty goals and was driven by her vision of success. Consider the details of Sally's career:

- She graduated from a prestigious university with honors.
- She is one of only three women in her company who holds an executive position.
- She serves on the board of directors at the children's hospital.
- She drives a nice car, owns a home, has a retirement plan, and has a son.

All along the way, Sally acquired skills and received accolades. Success gave her a feeling of significance and pride, motivating her to do more and to work even harder. She was able to climb the ladder of success because she was driven, loyal, and reliable. At first, being relied on made Sally feel valuable; being of service made her feel worthy.

Her family also relies on her. She visits her mom often and assists with her financial needs. She carries the burden of her mother's Alzheimer's for her siblings who are out of town and less involved. Again, it feels good to be needed and do the right thing, but she is running out of energy. Adding family stress to the demands of work is about to wear her down.

This is how we get roped into doing it all and sacrificing our own happiness. At the beginning, we're duped by a sense of accomplishment and the vision of what success and recognition will bring. Before long, however, we can't stop the do-it-all cycle. We blindly sacrifice true fulfillment for the sake of professional success or personal obligation until our dissatisfaction significantly impacts our well-being.

It's easy to do. Craving the approval of others, we sacrifice our own wants and needs. In the short term, accomplishing goals and serving others is satisfying—until resentment over the self-sacrifice starts to build. We have not been taught to care for ourselves, to love and respect ourselves along the way.

From a young age, we're taught to follow the rules, and this skill is pedaled as part of the happiness equation. Were you told, "Children are to be seen and not heard?" Society tells us, "Keep quiet and follow the rules." Few people take time to ponder the fallout from silencing the self and following the herd.

The truth is, generating your own happiness is a big, bold step—a departure from the expected rules society gives us. It will require you to give up worrying about what everyone else thinks. It will require you to change your definition of self-worth. In return, you will learn how to generate happiness for yourself and, ultimately, spread it to other people, too. You must simply give yourself permission to step away from the conventional.

Though Sally felt big emotions bubbling up as she pondered what was wrong, the last thing she wanted was to have a conversation about feelings—not with herself, and especially not with others. Many professionals avoid emotion and confrontation, so Sally had always avoided discussing any dissatisfaction or frustration. As a peacemaker, she had often accepted the short end of the stick to prevent upsets. She willed herself to snap out of it, telling herself she couldn't give in to this longing for change. Once she fully acknowledged the rut she was in, she wasn't sure what would happen.

She felt powerless, and her mind went to work to find answers—answers to alleviate the discomfort she was feeling with herself and the path her life had taken. It's quite natural for people to want to assign blame. Blaming the economy, the needy family member, that person who mistreated you, or the job with the bad boss is easier than doing work on ourselves. We rationalize, and we justify.

We ascribe blame to outside forces, and although you may not come up with a clear answer, you'll likely come up with plenty of reasons beyond your control to explain why you feel the way you do. When we focus on factors beyond our control, we feel disempowered. Feeling helpless, our "stuckness" starts to solidify, and we lose ourselves. We think something must be wrong with us, and the negativity soon becomes habitual. By dwelling on the people or circumstances to blame, we give up our control, creating the perception there's nothing we can do about our circumstances.

Not thinking to ask for help, we turn inward and rationalize, which reinforces our strong, limiting beliefs. We then live a limited life, making us even more unhappy. By validating why we're upset, we're creating and sustaining the belief we are defenseless and powerless, making the feeling of being stuck seem real. Thinking we are unable to do anything about our inner turmoil, we wait and hope for something external to change to make us happy.

But don't worry. We can unlearn this pattern. You are not the negative thinking in your head. You are not the limited beliefs you've conjured up. They are not real, but they are controlling your life and its outcomes.

Do you ever have a sense that there's something missing? Do you ever feel off track, like you're not living true to your purpose? Are you often spinning your wheels? Like Sally, are you stuck in a rut? Are you left feeling unfulfilled?

I have been there, overcome with the feeling that something is not quite right. The emotions stirred by your discontent are a sign, an indicator that you've disconnected from yourself. When you're disconnected, you cannot generate your own happiness. Generating happiness is an action that requires self-inquiry. You're not meant to be hopeless and helpless. Take time to ask yourself, *What is missing, and what would I like to have happen?* When you answer these questions, you will know where to get help and support.

Sally believed she couldn't count on anyone, which led to the thought, *No one really cares about me.* In her mind, the only person she could count on was herself, yet she felt at the mercy of life's circumstances. She wanted more in her career but would do anything to avoid conflict, to keep from inconveniencing a coworker or her boss. In her personal life, her dating life was unfulfilling, but she was embarrassed to admit it. After the divorce, she was hoping to meet the "right" one. Later, she justified her feelings of loneliness by thinking that "having it all" wasn't possible. In fact, she justified every area of life, making allowances for settling and rationalizing her compromises.

Alternately, at times she felt guilty about the level of success she had achieved. She sometimes wondered why she was lucky enough to have a high-paying job when others less fortunate struggled. Because, comparatively speaking, she seemed to have so much, she thought it was ungrateful to want more. Yet the ache was still there.

Can you relate? I can. You are not alone. Sally reached a low point before she considered change, but you don't have to hit rock bottom to say *enough is enough*. Are you ready to get unstuck?

LET'S PLAY:

- **WHERE IN YOUR LIFE ARE YOU FEELING UNINSPIRED?**

- **WHAT DO YOU SAY TO YOURSELF THAT MAKES YOU FEEL CONSTRAINED OR STUCK?**

CHAPTER 7

SALLY NUMBS HER PAIN

INSTEAD OF IDENTIFYING AND honoring what inspires her, Sally has been focusing on alleviating her unhappiness. From an early age, she learned to numb the pain. When things didn't go her way, when it seemed like nothing she could do was good enough, or when she was told to do something she didn't want to do, she didn't know how to cope with her negative emotional responses. So, she would find a way to forget. When she was cranky, she would escape by withdrawing and taking a nap. When she was bored, or didn't know what to do with herself, she would eat, turning to sugar and sweets.

When confronted with pain, people who are unable to generate their own happiness often indulge in pleasures that create a temporary, surface-level feeling of happiness. They drink, overeat, watch way too much TV, play video games, spend hours on social media, shop until they drop, or partake in unhealthy sexual activity, hoping these pleasures will distract them from feeling unhappy.

There are contradictory messages at play. We may sense that working less will give us a healthier work/life balance. However we are compelled to work more to make more money, thinking we will then be able to afford luxuries and pleasures that will take the edge off of our unhappiness. This is an empty pursuit. Many rich people discover they are still unhappy after buying whatever luxuries they desire. They then buy more to numb the growing emptiness, creating a thankless cycle.

We must instead ask ourselves, *What am I avoiding?* Could it be you indulge in feel-good activities to avoid feelings of unhappiness or to forget parts of yourself you don't like? We tend to think of addicts when we think of numbing feelings, but these are things we all do every day. In other words, you don't have to be an addict to suffer from the consequences of numbing behaviors.

You can't pick and choose the emotions you silence. Numbing negative emotions also dulls our experiences of joy, love, creativity, and the most fulfilling of life's experiences: connecting with others. Creating an altered state by taking over-the-counter or prescription drugs (like Ambien, Prozac, or Advil PM), drinking coffee, smoking (or vaping), or even being super busy alters your ability to experience true happiness.

You will notice I'm talking about activities our society says are normal, acceptable pursuits. Regular people, like you and me, have bought into the idea that staying busy or being a workaholic is good. We think caffeine and sleep meds are normal. But consider for a moment: could these habits be an escape of sorts? Do you find yourself working because you love it, or because you want to silence thoughts that creep in when you are quiet?

Why are we compelled to numb and avoid? Often, we want to distract ourselves from things like debt, being overweight, aging, disappointment over our lot in life, feelings of inadequacy, not having a sense of purpose, fear of uncertainty and instability, relationship issues, or loneliness. We want to feel more or less of something, rather than just feel what we're feeling.

What's the big deal, you might ask? According to the Center for Disease Control and Prevention, the following are the top-ten leading causes of death:

- Heart disease
- Cancer
- Chronic lower respiratory diseases
- Accidents (unintentional injuries)
- Stroke
- Alzheimer's disease
- Diabetes
- Influenza and pneumonia
- Nephritis, nephrotic syndrome, and nephrosis
- Intentional self-harm (suicide)

As you can see, the most lethal diseases are related to lifestyle choices, including poor diet, physical inactivity, and excessive alcohol use. The leading cause of accidental death (over automobile accidents) is drug overdose. The most common drugs involved in prescription overdose death include opioid pain killers, like Vicodin, OxyContin, and methadone. Prescription painkiller overdose deaths also often involve benzodiazepines, sedatives to induce sleep and relieve anxiety, like Xanex, Valium, and Ativan. Believe it or not, more people die from prescription drug overdoses than from heroin, cocaine, and methamphetamine use combined.

Drug abuse and dependency is a sign of how unhappy the world is and how important it is to learn to generate your own happiness. As we know, proactive and positive lifestyle choices contribute to our health, while poor choices increase our risk of disease and death.

Sally has had a couple of small health scares, but fortunately nothing really serious so far. The idea of being faced with a diagnosis that could prevent her from working and supporting her family is alarming, so she watches what she eats and takes daily vitamin supplements.

But why doesn't Sally know how to silence nagging thoughts that keep her up at night? Why won't she ask for support? Because she's been taught to serve and be self-sufficient, not to get help. Sally is addicted to responsibility and propriety, to taking care of everything and everyone but herself. She numbs her own worries and pain by being busy. She is scared to feel the messy feelings, so she does what she can to forget.

Often people avoid feeling emotions because they are uncomfortable with vulnerability. But feelings aren't bad; they're actually a clue to guide you to what you feel passionate about. In fact, I find that if I allow myself to notice and feel sadness, even if it's subtle, I can identify something that's near and dear to my heart. For instance, I feel sad when I see injustice; this points to my passion for equal rights for all of humanity and compassion for those less fortunate. Again, give yourself permission to feel and be open to whatever your feelings are guiding you to. What are the emotions trying to show you?

The more you engage in and appreciate the idiosyncrasies of life—instead of ignoring or running from them—the happier you will be. Life is full of wonder and awe. Start by letting go of preconceived notions of how things should be. Allow yourself to be curious. Ask yourself, *Am I happy, mad, sad, or afraid?* The goal is to increase your awareness so you will know what touches your heart. It will take practice because you are likely used to numbing. It will take time to begin questioning and tuning in to your feelings instead. But tuning in—instead of tuning out with pseudo pleasures—is an important part of generating your own happiness.

Consider this quote from Martin Seligman, a psychologist who has popularized positive thinking and endorses happiness as an integral part of wellness:

> *Relieving the states that make life miserable . . . has made building the states that make life worth living less of a priority. The time has finally arrived for a science that seeks to understand positive emotion, build strength and virtue, and provide guideposts for finding what Aristotle called the "good life."*

LET'S PLAY:

- ASK YOURSELF, *AM I MAD, SAD, ANGRY, OR AFRAID?* IF YOU HAVE DIFFICULTY IDENTIFYING HOW YOU FEEL, CONSIDER WHEN AND HOW YOU COULD BE NUMBING YOUR EMOTIONS.

- AS YOU ASK YOURSELF THE ABOVE QUESTION, PRACTICE LETTING GO OF ANY JUDGMENTS THAT COME UP. SIMPLY NOTICE HOW YOU FEEL, ALLOWING YOURSELF TO BE WITH YOUR FEELINGS–WITHOUT LABELING THE FEELINGS AS GOOD OR BAD.

CHAPTER 8

SERVING OR SACRIFICING?

SALLY COULD HAVE CHOSEN to numb by drinking too much, having an affair, or depending on prescription drugs. Her brand of numbing, however, was busyness, serving others, and going above and beyond at work—even if it meant denying her own needs. Because she had always been a good girl and had followed society's rules about working hard and achieving, Sally saw her productivity and efficiency as a plus. She felt needed at work and in her family relationships. She was so used to keeping busy that she didn't know any other way.

But here's the thing about serving others to the exclusion of self: without even knowing it, serving turns into sacrificing. At first you want to be helpful and then you are taken advantage of. Soon, you don't know how to say no and don't think no is an acceptable option. "No" is always an option.

Making a contribution is rewarding, yes, absolutely! In fact, doing good deeds produces positive emotion. But, are you contributing because it resonates with your soul, or are you contributing because you think you "have to" or "should"? Do you hope the sacrifice will make you a better person? Serving does not have to include sacrifice. If it doesn't make you feel warm and fuzzy, saying no is an option.

Many successful professionals, like Sally, turn service into sacrifice and become Gal Friday, which then turns into Gal Monday through Sunday. Can you relate? Are you the go-to gal who gets things done? Are you guilty of doing for everyone but yourself? And what if you're also a single parent like Sally? Of course you feel overwhelmed. Who wouldn't?

Let's think a bit more about making contribution. Who doesn't yearn to make a difference in the world? Who doesn't want a better life for their children? Doing for others or yearning to help feels good and lifts our spirits. However, we must notice when we are responding to a desire to serve the greatest and highest good versus making a sacrifice or simply trying not to rock the boat. Doing good by denying your own needs, wants, or self-expression cannot work long term. This is the gateway to a victim mentality.

You may be thinking, *I get it. I see where other people play the victim role.* But you're not a victim, right? You're tough and powerful, and you can do it all. However, just consider for a moment that you could be creating a victim mentality within yourself without realizing it, particularly if you stay too busy for reflection.

This process is subtle and happens gradually as we ignore our thoughts, desires, and feelings. In fact, we get to this place because we are not accustomed to identifying our emotional triggers and haven't learned to turn our perception of helplessness around. There's a lack of self-awareness as we continue to be the good girl, doing more and more for others or our company. Our society trains us to be unaware, teaching us to do what we're told. We learn to make decisions based on evaluations by teachers and employers.

To determine whether you are serving or sacrificing, ask yourself these questions:

- *Am I doing this hoping it helps my career?*
- *Am I doing this to appear to be a humanitarian?*

- *Am I doing this to help a friend?*
- *Am I doing this out of obligation?*
- *Do I want to do this?*

If you find yourself resentful or feeling like you don't have anyone you can count on, you could be stuffing your own emotions (numbing) or self-sacrificing. Trying always to do what's "best" by being submissive or holding back your own beautiful self-expression is not for the greatest good.

Remember, you play the most critical role in creating the greatest good in your life. Do you offer yourself acceptance and love? Do you allow genuine self-expression? Give yourself permission to be your most authentic self. And then shine. Most important, give yourself permission to feel what you are feeling. Stop the numbing and come to life with the wide range of feelings you've buried under the busyness and sacrifice.

What I am talking about may seem vague or unfamiliar. That's okay. You can start with whatever feelings come up for you and practice letting go of any self-judgment. You may also want to refer back to the unconditional love exercise suggested in Chapter Five. Try saying, "Even though I feel _____ (fill in the blank), I completely and uncondi- tionally love and accept myself." The upcoming "regeneration" process in Chapter Twelve is also helpful.

When you love and nurture yourself, you generate your own peace and happiness. And, if you long to make a difference in the world, you'll be even more successful as your inner resistance dissipates. Walk forward into your wonderful life, fully feeling all the emotions that make you unique.

LET'S PLAY:

- NOW THAT YOU KNOW HOW TO GET UNSTUCK, STOP NUMBING, AND FEEL YOUR FEELINGS, IT'S TIME TO IDENTIFY AND ACKNOWLEDGE WHAT YOUR SOUL WANTS. WHAT LIGHTS YOU UP? WHAT WOULD YOU DO IF YOU WERE ONLY CONSIDERING *YOUR* PASSIONS AND *YOUR* WISHES?

- IN WHAT AREAS OF LIFE HAS YOUR SERVING TURNED TO SACRIFICE? LET GO OF SACRIFICING AND DREAM BIG.

CHAPTER 9

⌒

SALLY HAS BOUNDARY ISSUES

BOUNDARIES CAN PHYSICALLY MARK the limits of an area, indicating this far and no further. You may have also heard about boundaries in relationships—setting limits for how another person can treat you. Establishing appropriate boundaries can be the foundation that supports us in fulfilling our hearts' desires and grand purpose in life. But I'd like to tweak how we typically think of "boundaries." An aspect of boundaries that is not often discussed is self-knowledge. To know where to set a healthy boundary, you first have to understand your own feelings and the feelings others elicit in you.

Sally has been told she needs boundaries, but she doesn't really know what that means. For Sally, the idea of setting boundaries conjures up the notion of putting her foot down about certain things. She does not equate setting boundaries with generating happiness. In fact, setting boundaries doesn't sound healthy or happy at all; it sounds more like confrontation, which she avoids as it adds to her stress.

Because she dislikes confrontation, Sally always says yes to family and coworkers, even when she wants to say no. Sally works even when she's sick. She doesn't know when to say no or how to honor the limits that would keep her soul healthy. Sally doesn't have boundaries because she hasn't established what is important to her. Without a clear vision of what she must have to be happy, she doesn't know how to identify and say no to things that contradict her own needs and desires. Sally's self-knowledge is poor.

Sally believes it's important to be perceived as someone who is nice, a team player. Sadly, she is hoping to please people who don't really care whether she is nice or not. They just want to get their work done and have come to depend on her help.

She is a workaholic, which generally implies a person who loves his work. However, Sally works to meet obligations and keep up her reputation. On the job and in her personal life, she is consumed with what people think of her. She often wonders whether people like her or not—and this fixation feeds her need to do more. A workaholic people pleaser, Sally has created her own brand of unhappiness.

Sally works long hours because she believes it's the right thing to do. She needs to provide for herself and her son, and she wants to be seen as a woman of her word. She was taught at a young age that if you want something, you have to work hard for it.

Everyone has faith and trust in Sally; that's why they keep asking her for help. They know she will never say no, but this is leadership without appropriate boundaries. Sally allows her fear of conflict to limit her and create a sense of being trapped.

People like Sally have a tendency to be people pleasers, but they almost never know it. They lack clear boundaries and look for validation from the outside world. They think they are responsible because they are constantly doing for everyone else, but they aren't being responsible to themselves. They don't practice appropriate self-care.

In fact, their inability to say no often results in self-neglect. Rather than own your greatness and power, do you ever downgrade your greatness, portraying the fake humility you think others expect? Do you ever make sacrifices that you know don't support your well-being?

Sally is an overachiever and thinks getting things done will bring her relief. The competitive part of her says, *Nobody is going to outwork me.* She attributes her success to years of perseverance and "paying her dues," coming in early and working late. She makes a point of being the first to arrive and last to leave so her employees don't resent her. Sally considers her work ethic and willingness to help others as a badge of honor. Being the heroine feeds her ego, but the satisfaction it brings doesn't feed her soul.

There is a big difference between feeding your soul and feeding your ego when it comes to generating your own happiness. Your soul is the keeper of your happiness. Your ego is the keeper of struggle.

When you continue to keep up appearances but lack appropriate boundaries, you may look good to others, but you will feel unhappy inside. You have tied your happiness to ego accomplishments, not authentic soul desires. Having appropriate boundaries is about answering and honoring what feels good on a soul level.

When Sally prioritizes work, she is giving her happiness away. Most, if not all, of her social activities revolve around business or family obligations. She manages to get in a workout twice a week, but it's seldom fun. She makes the time for exercise because she has a certain image to uphold. Her home is neat and orderly because of her impulse to make everything perfect and maintain appearances. Staying on top of it all is exhausting.

Up to this point, Sally's boundaries have been defined by what she's been told she needs to do to make it in the world and get along with others. She's been living out what she's been told will make her happy (earning a good living, owning nice things, providing for her family, giving back to the community). Instead of pursuing what would make her genuinely happy, she's been consumed by doing what others have taught her will eventually lead to happiness. Thus, she is living someone else's ideal of happiness, not hers. Without even knowing it, Sally is allowing herself to be limited by these invisible barriers. If this is what you're doing, can you see why you're so unhappy?

If you ask Sally about her boundary issues, she'll probably admit to letting people take advantage of her by dumping extra work on her plate or borrowing money and not paying her back, but she thinks those compromises don't really affect her. What people don't know about Sally is that she's not happy about some of the situations she's found herself in, "doing what it takes" to win a lucrative contract for the company. She's learned that many business deals are made after hours and after many drinks. She hasn't set healthy boundaries in this area either, but she doesn't want to create drama by refusing to go along with the wine-and-dine culture.

Yet setting appropriate boundaries isn't the act of preventing certain circumstances. Nor is it the ability to manipulate or force others to behave in a certain way to protect yourself. Setting boundaries means knowing yourself, what self-care you need, and what feeds your soul. It is creating a structure to support a happier and more fulfilling life. Setting appropriate boundaries means you know yourself and what is important to you. You protect what lights you up and set a limit on things that don't.

Most people fail to set their own boundaries because they are following preset societal standards, trusting there's some one-size-fits-all formula for happiness, but healthy, appropriate boundaries are a result of knowing and loving yourself. They require knowing your distinct needs.

What Sally actually needs is to be true to what speaks to her soul, but she hasn't identified what she really wants because she doesn't know how. Instead, she's been asking others, "What do you think?"

Ultimately, Sally is unhappy because she lacks a deep feeling of purpose. She doesn't know how to connect with her unique calling; she doesn't know how to pursue what will make her happy. She has pursued "success" by maintaining a certain status and following other people's opinions, but she hasn't asked herself what she really wants. Because she never listens to her inner guidance, she doesn't know what boundaries are appropriate to set with others. She hasn't yet given herself permission to have faith and trust in herself.

I know firsthand what it feels like to live without firm boundaries. I've been guilty of burning the candle at both ends and feeling buried under obligations. When I continued to do and do, without considering my own happiness, I eventually felt trapped, like I didn't have any options. I finally realized I had to develop more self-awareness and take my power back. I had to own how I was giving my happiness away and blaming others. I also had to overcome the limiting self-talk and own my greatness. This is an ongoing practice and art.

Once I embraced myself 100 percent and really took a look at my life, I discovered what truly made me happy. What I found was that happiness is generated by action; it's not a reaction. It is something you become, not find. You don't find happiness; you become happiness.

Happiness doesn't just magically happen as a result of acquiring wealth, taking a vacation, or being everyone's favorite. Happiness is an action you take, a state of being. It requires discernment, as in listening intently for the truth in your soul and then creating a plan to support it. This is how your boundaries grow naturally, and this is the start of producing your own happiness.

However, for most people, Sally included, the issue with setting boundaries isn't about controlling must haves or eliminating what they can't stand, nor is it about willpower. It's not even about being strong enough to say no, although Sally seldom considers the option to decline. In fact, trying to control what you perceive as wrong and forcing it to fit within specific parameters will set you up for disappointment. To quote psychiatrist Carl Jung, "What you resist not only persists, but will grow in size."

The transformational element with boundaries is identifying and asking for what you want. Most people know what they *don't* want but seldom identify their core needs, like love and connection. What's missing isn't a defined boundary line to prevent others from crossing, like many tend to think. What's missing, if you lack boundaries, is the practice of self-inquiry, self-love, honor, and support.

With self-inquiry comes the ability to see when you are living inside imaginary barriers and self-limiting beliefs. Once you have this awareness, you will be able to step out of the box and generate something new for yourself. Sometimes insight is all you really need to make the "stuckness" magically disappear. Other times, it takes a little push. With practice, you'll be able to discern which approach is appropriate and allow yourself the joy of honoring this internal wisdom.

As you can now see clearly, unhappiness occurs as a result of what you're telling yourself—the "shoulds" and obligations you have followed mindlessly. Anger and resentment stem from the inability to ask for what you need. Genuine, sustainable happiness and fulfillment comes from identifying and honoring what yearns to be expressed deep in your core.

Instead of focusing on what's not permissible or what is expected, redirect your attention to what's really important to you. I believe you'll discover a grand desire to expand your capacity to love and be loved, but the true joy comes in discovering and expressing what that looks like for you specifically.

But first, you need to identify what that is for you. Don't fret if you don't yet know your deepest desire; you can choose, then change your mind later if you wish. The more you trust your inner compass, the easier it gets. And, even though it may seem like it sometimes, you are not alone. Support is available. Asking for support can make you feel vulnerable if you're not accustomed to it, yet support is what you deserve. It's time to build a life worth living.

LET'S PLAY:

- WHAT DEEPLY MOVES YOU, INSPIRES YOU, OR MOTI-VATES YOU TO ACTION?

- ACKNOWLEDGE YOUR GREATNESS. WHAT ABOUT YOUR-SELF DO YOU ESPECIALLY VALUE AND APPRECIATE?

- NOTE AREAS IN YOUR LIFE THAT COULD BENEFIT FROM ACQUIRING SUPPORT. FOR IDEAS AND FREE RESOURCES, VISIT WWW.GENERATINGYOUROWNHAPPINESS.COM.

- ASK FOR SUPPORT IN AN AREA THAT IS MEANINGFUL TO YOU. ALLOW YOUR GREATNESS TO SHINE.

CHAPTER 10

~~~⌒~~~

TAKING OWNERSHIP

YOU MAY RECOGNIZE SOME of the patterns that have contributed to your unhappiness, but what steps ought you take to generate sustainable happiness? Generating your own happiness requires being responsible for yourself, which is an ongoing practice.

Some people call it "personal responsibility" or "self-responsibility." I also like to use the term "ownership" for this concept. What exactly is self-responsibility? It means being accountable for your actions, taking ownership of the outcome of your decisions. Being responsible is one of the signs of becoming an adult. While some associate self-responsibility with performing duty and accepting blame, this interpretation gives the term a negative connotation.

The more hopeful truth is that being self-responsible and taking owner-ship gives you command of your happiness. It makes you the source of your own life, which alleviates unnecessary suffering and creates peace. It gives you access to your creative abilities. In short, being self-responsible means being self-empowered. When you are empowered, you can generate virtually anything your heart desires.

Think of resolving a business problem or customer complaint. Fixating on blame will backfire every time. Taking responsibility is forward thinking. Someone new to business may have the propensity to wait for someone else with authority. A leader is responsible. Asking yourself "What can I do?" allows you to make a decision and progress.

As we grow, we learn to master our abilities. Think back to when you learned to tie your shoes or ride a bike. Once you got it, those abilities became natural. Like riding a bike, generating happiness may seem challenging at first, but once you acquire and persistently practice what I call "happiness mindfulness", you will have this ability for the rest of your life. It's an ever-changing and growing capacity that you govern when you choose to do so.

Generating your own happiness is the art of being aware in the present moment, effectively identifying what you want, and acting on behalf of your desire. It's discerning the feelings and beliefs that either empower you or disempower you. This kind of insightful engagement will create a sense of fulfillment and aliveness.

Don't worry if you feel you are far from that state now. Discovering what is not working means you are taking the first and most important step: becoming actively engaged.

If you've already applied some of what you've been learning in this book, you may have experienced more curiosity, awe, and appreciation for being human and experiencing emotion. Congratulations! You are beginning to generate your own happiness. With a small step forward, we shift our outcomes. Continuing to take action builds momentum.

Most often, change doesn't happen in one giant leap. Rather, it's a series of small wins that add up to notable progress. In fact, we often underestimate how much change can occur from making micro-fine adjustments.

Mastering self-responsibility and discovering how to empower yourself is the first step toward generating happiness. When you claim your new, more empowered mindset, it's a big win. You may want to cheer for yourself.

Children celebrate often, but are taught not to brag. As a result, the natural pride response is stifled in adults. We've learned to suppress or diminish our enthusiasm for the small triumphs that create big wins.

Allow the kid within you to celebrate your victories. You will unlock more wins that, in turn, create more victory and success. You are giving yourself approval often sought from others. You are learning to revere the power within.

Too often, people read a book but don't actively implement the knowledge gained. They wait for someone else to make them change. Rather than tapping into their own power and taking personal responsibility, they are content to wait. Have you heard the story about the man who prayed to God to rescue him from the flood?

A terrible storm came into a town and local officials sent out an emergency warning that the riverbanks would soon overflow and flood the nearby homes. They ordered everyone in the town to evacuate. A man heard the warning and decided to stay, saying to himself, *I have faith that if I am in danger, God will send a divine miracle to save me.*

The man stood on his porch, watching the water rise up to the steps. A man with a canoe called to him, "Hurry and come into my canoe. The waters are rising quickly!" But the man said, "No, thanks. God will save me."

The floodwaters rose. Water poured into the man's living room, and he retreated to the second floor. A police motorboat came by, and the officers saw him at the window. "We will come up and rescue you!" they shouted. But the man refused, waving them off and saying, "Use your time to save someone else! I have faith that God will save me!"

The flood waters rose higher and higher, and the man had to climb up to his rooftop. He prayed to God to help him. A helicopter spotted him and dropped a rope ladder. A rescue officer came down the ladder and pleaded with the man, "Grab my hand, and I will pull you up!" But the man refused, folding his arms tightly to his body. "No, thank you! God will save me!" Shortly after, the floodwaters swept the man away, and he drowned.

When the man reached heaven and stood before God, he said, "I put all of my faith in you. Why didn't you come and save me?" God responded, "Son, I sent you a warning. I sent you two boats and a helicopter. What more were you looking for?"

What does this story teach? We seldom pay attention to the obvious steps we can take to rescue ourselves because we are looking for a higher, more profound answer.

Generating happiness is really not that complicated. Yet, we make life complicated because we do not proactively focus on self-awareness and happiness. Instead, we prioritize a bunch of stuff that doesn't fulfill us. Then we wonder why we're in a rut. We may send up a prayer for help, yet we continue to do the same thing over again, hoping for a different result. We become the man in the flood. We wait on divine intervention, rather than focusing our attention inward, where we have the most power.

Is it possible you've been complicating your life by waiting for some magical solution to your problems? Have you passed up opportunities or neglected the things that bring you true joy because you've been following rules or being critical? How often do we miss the blessings in life because they haven't come in the shape or form we expected? This is the "man-in-the-flood syndrome."

Is it possible that you miss out on enjoying happiness in life because you've been trying to numb the pain of emotional wounds from your past? Can you see any areas where you have given away your power? Hint: since picking up this book, have you assigned blame, giving away your power by putting the blame on other people or outside circumstances? Have you made "sexy excuses" in your mind?

Sexy excuses are the evidence we find to validate our limiting beliefs—they are the external variables we blame for our unhappiness. I call them "sexy" because they are hard to resist; they are seductive and cunning but leave us powerless. Without knowing it, we get drawn into believing they are real. Soon, we think there is nothing we can do to overcome them. Believing sexy excuses prevents us from generating happiness and having a life we love. They make us think outside circumstances are keeping us stuck, and they excuse us from being one-hundred percent authentic. As long as we give in to them, sexy excuses will dampen self-expression and keep us from taking risks and loving the full experience of life.

So, have you been blaming others or believing sexy excuses about your current circumstances? If you have, this is a great opportunity! This is a chance to become more self-responsible and claim your happiness. Taking ownership and being able to turn blame or a complaint into curious inquiry and action is powerful. When you practice being mindful and letting go of judgments, you'll notice a shift in how you feel.

If you're still unable to identify what you're saying or believing that is, in effect, creating your unhappiness, consider your complaints and notice the flood of "make wrong" that comes up. Who or what are you judging, making wrong, or blaming?

Don't let the short-lived satisfaction of the ego-self, which loves to be right and make others wrong, fool you. Complaining about others and fault-finding are as draining as sexy excuses and the blame game. Though you may feel temporarily smug and justified, these tactics ultimately have a bigger cost than reward.

But you are now empowered to avoid this. Let's examine how to relate to self-responsibility and get past any resistance. Join me as we develop a template for long-lasting happiness.

To begin, notice how you feel when you hear the word "responsibility." Notice how the idea of being more personally responsible, of shoring up your boundaries, usually conjures up a response that is anything but light, fun, and happy. Do you associate the word "responsible" with blame and obligation? Most people associate responsibility with performing a duty, taking control, or taking the blame . . . then we wonder why we don't feel motivated and inspired.

My guess is that you have no problem taking responsibility in a general sense. It's likely you are accountable for pretty much everything and everyone in your immediate circle. Is that true? But are you also being self-responsible in a caring and loving way? Are you comfortable looking within and confidently living as the source of your life?

I'm sure you've heard plenty of quotes related to self-empowerment. Let's use the following Jim Rohn quote as an example: "You must take personal responsibility. You cannot change the circumstances, the seasons, or the wind, but you can change yourself." How does this thought make you feel? If you aren't in touch with or able to follow your inner compass, do you get a little uncomfortable with being told to be responsible?

Because the word "responsibility" can have a negative connotation, the proper message isn't always getting through. It's valuable to understand that our subconscious associations generate our emotional responses, our happiness or unhappiness. We want to create a positive default response to responsibility, rather than negative, because we are most empowered when in a positive mental state.

Why must we each be responsible and understand our inner compass? Many people reach a certain level of professional success by pulling themselves up by their boot straps, numbing the pain or discomfort, and doing whatever it takes to reach their goal, but when they finally achieve what they wanted, they aren't happy. Let's take a look at your life and where you are "responsible".

Do you ever feel resentful? Are you guilty of putting everyone else's needs above your own? If so, it's no wonder you feel uninspired. I understand how you feel—many of us have been in that place at one time.

Most people think being responsible means being reliable and accountable, busting your hump, and getting the project completed at all costs. If you're in the professional world, you're probably already giving it your all, pleasing the company while trying to maintain balance and meeting the expectations of your family. If you're doing it all, your responsibility level is overwhelming.

But this kind of soul-crushing responsibility is not what Jim Rohn refers to in the quote. Rather, he's referring to self-responsibility, being aware of and harnessing your own initiative, authority, and ability to choose. But can you see how we can rush to the other, more draining interpretation of responsibility without realizing it?

Again, you must be aware of your subconscious thoughts if you hope to shift your happiness levels. Happiness is not possible if you are ruled by your subconscious, default thoughts. You must instead direct your focus with clear intention—because thoughts (what you're telling yourself) lead to emotions; emotions lead to action (or, in many cases, inaction); and action leads to results.

If you aren't seeing the results you want, it's because you are allowing limiting beliefs to rule you or are reacting to a trigger, an automatic association that brings to mind an old wound. Many people will do almost anything to avoid these painful responses. While some numb the pain to the point of debilitation, others may turn their whole life upside down running from it. An automatic reaction to a negative association always ends in more pain, whereas happiness comes from focused, deliberately positive thoughts.

You are responsible for your self-talk, your decisions, and the actions you take. This is valuable to understand: you can be responsible for your happiness by being aware and mindful. Being mindful means focusing your awareness on the present moment. It is calmly and courageously acknowledging and accepting your feelings, thoughts, and bodily sensations. Without awareness and mindfulness, you allow the preprogramming of the subconscious to run your reactions and, thus, your life.

LET'S PLAY:

- IN WHAT AREAS ARE YOU GUILTY OF HAVING "MAN-IN-THE-FLOOD SYNDROME"? ARE YOU WAITING FOR A BOLT FROM THE BLUE, WHEN WHAT YOU REALLY NEED TO DO IS TAKE ONE SMALL STEP FORWARD?

- WHAT SEXY EXCUSES ARE YOU TELLING YOURSELF? WHAT TRUTH CAN YOU USE TO COMBAT THESE EXCUSES?

- WHO OR WHAT DO YOU LOVE TO "MAKE WRONG"? IN WHAT AREAS ARE YOU COMPLAINING AND JUDGING? HOW CAN YOU TAKE OWNERSHIP?

CHAPTER 11

POSITIVE OR NEGATIVE?

SO FAR, I'VE ENDEAVORED to grab your attention, redirect your focus, and point you to a mindful place. My goal is to help you recognize the traps of unhappiness so you can be aware and empowered. When you practice self-responsibility and actively engage every aspect of your life from this place, you have the power to create genuine happiness for yourself.

To modify self-talk and default attitudes, you must catch yourself in the act of turning negative. This requires self-awareness; you must pay attention to you. Observing the chatter in your mind helps you understand the emotional turbulence you create. For example, you may find yourself going from short-lived excitement to feeling horribly defeated and rundown, both physically and emotionally. If you want a different result, you must say something different, and your mind and body will create it right then.

If you're unhappy, ask yourself, *What am I saying that I'm believing to be true?* If you are experiencing sadness, anger, frustration, or a similar negative emotion, there is a limiting belief behind it.

Most people feel stuck when faced with dilemmas that have no obvious solution. Most automatically believe they don't have what's needed, so they fall into old behaviors and experience more unhappiness. This is how we lose motivation, get stuck in a negative mindset, and feel like giving up. Believe it or not, most people who think their role is to be "responsible" will automatically think of that in a negative way, feeling as if they don't have choices.

You may not realize how often you default to some form of "make wrong" or blame, creating a negative, victim mentality. How often do you complain, either to yourself or out loud? Remember, the more you tell yourself something and find ways to validate it, the more you believe it to be true.

However, you can retool your mind. It can work for you or against you. Which do you want to grow, positive or negative thoughts?

When you find yourself identifying a problem, as we did in chapter ten, the first thing you want to do is take responsibility for what you're saying to yourself. By looking inward and choosing where you direct your focus, you are being intentional, rather than defaulting to triggers and past associations.

This is where being self-responsible is valuable. Although we don't usually recognize it, the mind has a built-in negativity bias, and we tend to ruminate on unpleasant events more than happy ones. In fact, negativity is all around us. The media is known for breeding negativity. Even our loved ones can dwell on their unhappiness and deflect that gloom to us.

Obviously, focusing on negativity or complaining about the things you wish you could change won't make you happy—neither will trying to change your loved ones. In fact, this approach will only increase the negativity, for what you resist persists.

You cannot control everything that happens in the world, but you can determine how you respond to it, and your reaction directly impacts your happiness. You must be willing to give up judgment to engage fully in life and embrace happiness.

As you know, if a person focuses on his strengths, achievements, and accomplishments, he will see the world open up; he will enjoy astonishing opportunities. This positive outlook becomes positive energy, increased creativity, a stronger sense of competence, and a competitive edge or what Shawn Achor, one of the world's leading experts on the connection between happiness and success, coined as the "Happiness Advantage". The individual with empowering self-talk can say, "Bring it on. I can handle it. I am able!" and results follow.

The magic to having a life you love is to claim it and then create it. You are the source for your happiness; you hold the key. So be deliberate in your actions and generate your own happiness. Be deliberate in what you tell yourself because our perceptions and experience of reality originates in our thoughts and feelings. Everything we do is a result of what we tell ourselves, which produces corresponding emotions. Think about being self-responsible as being able to check in with what you are telling yourself and choose powerfully what you say, think, and do. Being self-responsible means you know how to practice mindfulness and choose to operate in a positive mindset so that you can generate your own happiness. What will you manifest in your life?

The issue for most is that we don't deliberately and proactively create support for our ongoing happiness. Instead, we seek out what we hope will make us happy—not what actually lights us up or gives us a sense of purpose and fulfillment. Most people focus their attention and energy on changing the external force they think is making them unhappy. They blame other people or circumstances, but this has never gotten anyone anywhere.

For example, most women think if they lose weight, then they will be happy, but they may have a slow metabolism or genetics working against them. Or some think they have to make more money and get out of debt to be happy. Again, this could be nearly impossible because of personal obstacles. I could go on and on. However, it is this pitfall—the focus on the negative, outside forces we're unhappy about that prevents us from having what we truly want.

Like Sally, most people don't tap into and trust their inner guidance (the divine/God/universal wisdom). Generating authentic, sustainable happiness involves identifying what your soul wants and building a structure to honor and support what warms your heart. You will be amazed by the opportunities that seem to magically appear when you're in a positive mindset and looking for the good.

Now, don't get me wrong. All disappointment and struggle won't magically disappear by adjusting your attitude. Turbulence is inevitable. I like to describe struggle as part of the adventure of living life to the fullest.

Pleasure does not require any skill. It feels good in the moment, but the downside is it doesn't last or involve growth. To experience lasting enjoyment and fulfillment, you must grow as you struggle and overcome. In other words, the obstacles we face are part of what makes life satisfying. Those who avoid challenges, rather than embracing them, are seldom happy. Generating your own happiness is an ongoing process of facing and growing through life's challenges.

Happiness needs to be cultivated to grow. Happy people don't wait for happiness to land in their laps. Genuinely happy people learn to touch their own hearts and souls as they trust and honor themselves. They experience a deep sense of knowing and practice the art of generating happiness as they focus on the positive—even during times of struggle.

Let me give you an example of self-responsibility from my own life. In the midst of writing this book, I seized the opportunity to turn my negative thoughts into a positive experience.

It seemed like everything and everyone was keeping me from writing. Business was pouring in for my lighting company, which meant everyone was working full force to stay on top of the work load, including me. To make matters worse, we were short-handed, due to the termination of an employee who held a critical role.

It was apparent we had a hole in the boat if being short one employee meant I personally had to pick up so much slack. We had noticed the need for more employees earlier, so it wasn't especially enjoyable to bear the brunt of having put off hiring.

I also wasn't loving my daily commute or my role as stepmother. I found myself snapping at the kids, saying things like, "Being a stepmother is a thankless job", as I anticipated their complaints about dinner—a meal I had prepared after I was already exhausted from working double-duty. I was tired, plus discouraged because I hadn't made the time to write.

It was time to be self-responsible for myself and my negative attitude. How could I take ownership versus be at the mercy of my seemingly busy schedule? I had to do some self-inquiry. What were my own sexy excuses, which seemed so valid because I was living them as if they were true? I asked, "What am I saying to myself?"

I was telling myself my book was less important than my lighting company because the company fed employees' families and the book was my personal project. I also believed I had all the responsibility (duty) to help support the family I married into, without having any say about the kids. After all, I was the wife, not the parent.

Notice how I said, "the family", not "my family." We will dive into the subtleties of language in the next chapter. Our choice of words can have quite an impact on our emotions—and those of our recipients.

The kids have an active mother and father who try to make everything work. The last thing they needed, I felt, was my contradictory opinions about parenting. Of course, I still managed to give my husband a piece of my mind on occasion, only to experience regret as I would tell myself I should be above that kind of cruddy behavior. Even when I was biting my lip, I was saying something contemptuous in my mind about pretty much everything. Needless to say, I was not happy. I was physically and mentally exhausted, feeling stuck in a negative place.

However, as a result of my self-inquiry, I could see—beneath my complaints—that I was living as though I didn't make a difference. I knew my assessment was correct when this thought made sadness flood my body. I had hit a nerve.

From the time I was a child, all I ever wanted was for people to be happy. When I allow myself to feel, I know two things to be true: I want people to love each other, and I want to make a contribution to this world. Yet, I was sidetracked, consumed by the idea that if this book didn't get finished, no one would know or care about that, other than me. I was discounting my ability to contribute and abandoning my desire to make a difference—with this book and also with my personal influence. I was withholding a major part of myself (the generous, loving part) from the humans with whom I share a home. When I looked at what I was saying to myself, it was no wonder I was feeling uninspired.

So, what did I do? I took a deep breath and allowed myself to be with the sadness. I acknowledged the tender part of me that cares about people. What a beautiful thing! Next, since I was at my lighting company when I had this ah-ha moment, I had a brief conversation with my employees. My right-hand man looked uncomfortable as he saw my emotions. When he tried to shush me, I acknowledged what he was seeing and told him it was a good thing, letting him know that nothing tragic had happened, these were good emotions.

I shared openly about my book and what it meant to me. I also told them I loved them and thanked them for being part of our team. Yep. I said, "I love you", to my employees, and, as of now, they haven't sued me or anything. We were already pretty close, but it's amazing how much more engaged they are with each other now.

I also had a conversation with my husband and apologized for my recent behavior. I explained what I had been telling myself and acknowledged how it had affected him. The conversation seemed to go especially well, but the next evening after putting the kids to bed my husband told me his daughter had voiced that she didn't want to come to our house when he picked up the kids for our weekend. I think he tried to sugarcoat the story a little, but I was pretty sure his daughter was uncomfortable with me.

Up until this point, it seemed like both of my husband's children were amazingly accepting of having me as their stepmother. They were both loving towards me. Was this just the beginning of difficult times ahead?

The next day, to my surprise, my husband's daughter opted to stay home with me rather than go with her dad and brother to baseball practice. I was a little nervous, but I didn't let it stop me. I took a deep breath and reminded myself to come from a place of authenticity. Since I had already had a conversation with her in my head, I started by asking if she had ever had that experience. We both chuckled a little.

Then I was just really honest. I told her I had been biting my lip, telling myself it wasn't my place to talk about certain things. She responded, telling me I could talk about anything, that her mom's boyfriend did that all the time. I laughed and then explained I was passionate about her feeling loved, accepted, and comfortable in her own skin. I told her I didn't want anyone to be discriminated against for any reason—regardless of race, sexual orientation, or religion. I also admitted that, even though I didn't know what she was being taught at school, I had this idea that people might be trying to teach her not to be accepting. I explained this kind of behavior came from fear.

We ended up taking the dogs for a walk and having the most amazing, open dialog. She asked me all kinds of questions, and I answered the best I could. Since then, it's been much more enjoyable to come home. It's like a cloud has lifted, and there is no longer an elephant in our living room. I can't believe how long I discounted myself as a stepmother. By losing focus of what was essential for my own fulfillment, I generated *un*happiness, not just for myself but also for those I love. I was letting my negative, limiting beliefs triumph—until I got in touch with my inner dialogue and reminded myself that beneath every upset lies an opportunity for something wonderful.

When I inquired within and allowed myself to feel what I had been subconsciously trying to numb, I was able to see my own blind spot. I could see the lies I was telling myself. I was then able to acknowledge the deeper emotion around feeling like I didn't make a difference; I could see the impact self-doubt was having on me and on those in my life. It took courage to be brave and own my deepest fears.

While it was clear I needed to have a conversation with my coworkers, husband, and stepdaughter, I was still nervous. However, sometimes you just need to have faith and be willing to take a risk. The results were greater than I could have imagined. I was able to express what was important to me and also contribute to and deepen my relationships. Who doesn't want that?

LET'S PLAY:

- WHAT NEGATIVE CHATTER IS PLAYING IN YOUR MIND? NOTICE AN AREA WHERE YOU FEEL DISEMPOWERED AND ASK YOURSELF, "WHAT AM I SAYING TO MYSELF?"

- ARE YOU BLAMING OTHERS AND GROWING RESENTFUL OF YOUR SITUATION? HOW CAN YOU CHOOSE TO CHANGE YOUR NEGATIVE EMOTION INTO POSITIVE ACTION?

- IS THERE A CONVERSATION YOU NEED TO HAVE WITH A LOVED ONE TO COME CLEAN ABOUT YOUR FEELINGS OF FRUSTRATION OR BLAME?

CHAPTER 12

A MENTAL RENOVATION: YOUR WORDS MATTER

YOU'VE PROBABLY HEARD MORE than once that your thoughts create your reality. This is not a new concept, but I want to help you identify how you personally contribute to the creation of your perceived reality. This is valuable to understand because humans are meaning-making machines. Where things fall apart, or how things come together, depends on where you focus your attention and what you are saying to yourself.

We naturally interpret everything at an exceptional rate of speed. It only takes seconds for you to destroy or empower yourself. Your brain is constantly assessing and reacting, while that voice in your head is repeating and reinforcing the messages the brain constructs. These messages shape your perceptions and beliefs.

If you are thinking something along the lines of, *It's an incredibly beautiful day, and I'm lucky to be alive*, you are probably feeling grateful and perky. Positive thinking creates a sense of aliveness, and you will be engaged with the world around you. When in this state, you're more likely to connect with people as they respond to your positive energy. When we're contributing to others in this way, we feel a sense of purpose. However, if we're thinking, *Nothing is going the way it should*, we feel discouraged, lethargic, disappointed, sad, and frustrated—not fully alive or hopeful.

Let's consider what Sally likely says when feeling stuck:

- "I have to get this project done."
- "I never have the help I need."
- "No one is competent or dependable."
- "I never have enough time."
- "I don't know how to get ahead."
- "I have to carry the entire burden."
- "No one really cares about me."
- "I need more *me* time."
- "I can't go on like this."

Did you notice Sally's disempowering language? Her word choice creates a sense of helplessness.

- I never
- I don't know how
- I have to
- No one
- I need
- I can't

It's interesting how vocabulary is both generated by and exerts influence on the brain. The bundle of nerves at the base of the skull is called the reticular activating system (RAS), which acts as a filter between your conscious and subconscious mind. Consciously, you can process forty bits of data per second, yet your subconscious mind can process forty million bits per second. Your subconscious mind is a million times more powerful than your conscious mind. I like to think of the RAS as the gatekeeper at the front desk, filtering which sales presentations get through.

Your word choice communicates to your subconscious what is important to focus on and filter for. Unless you actively engage your conscious mind to direct your attention, your subconscious mind will automatically process ninety-five percent or more of our decisions, actions, emotions, and behaviors, based on preprogrammed perceptions. These perceptions were mostly acquired from early, formative observation of and response to parents, teachers, siblings, and the community.

Positive, empowering language triggers your reticular activating system to find opportunities and solutions. It can, in turn, help you realize your best intentions. This is why affirmations and visualization exercises are so effective. Your word choice is an essential element in generating your own happiness. When you catch yourself feeling stuck, notice what you're saying to yourself and use it as an opportunity to create something new.

A "renovation" is a fundamental practice to change your perception of your current circumstances and generate specific outcomes. You can also think of it as a do-over or "mental renovation." Ask yourself what you can change about what you are saying that will generate the feeling that you have options. We create our experiences through our language and our thoughts (self-talk). What you say is what you are focusing on. As we know, what we focus on and put our energy into grows. Your life is a reflection of what you are saying and thinking. Your story and beliefs create your happiness or unhappiness, which creates your perceived reality.

Okay, so maybe you already know this, but knowing this and practicing it are two different things. This is where practice *does* make perfect. You are either going to practice using empowering language or settle for disempowering language. Whichever you choose will generate happiness or unhappiness, thereby creating your life.

The negative emotions that coincide with disempowering language are cues, signals that you're not happy, and it's almost impossible to be happy when you're disconnected from your true self. When you recognize the cues, you can turn the negative emotion around and take your power back by changing your language. It's really that simple.

It's helps to be mindful of this. So often, we get stuck in an unhappy place and focus (sometimes for years!) on what we don't like or what we want to change externally. This negative fixation tells the subconscious mind to validate the bad emotions, not to turn them around. We stay stuck ruminating on the negative story we are telling ourselves. Noticing your internal dialogue can alert you to be aware. What you're feeling is real, but the meaning you've made up is not.

Our emotional and physical responses are a result of what we're saying to ourselves, so use discernment. Notice what you're saying and the corresponding feelings and emotions you create. Noticing takes practice, but the more you do it, the easier it becomes to turn around negative language and reverse the sense of being stuck.

For example, we've all used the following phrases: "I don't know how"; "They always"; "They make me"; "He needs to"; "I need to"; "It's because"; "I have to"; "I can't"; "I'm too"; or "I'm not enough." You can pick your demon: "I'm too busy, too tired, too old." Or, "I'm not smart enough", "not connected enough." We also tend to use extreme language like, "always", "never", and "no one", which further emphasizes the sense of being powerless.

With disempowering language comes negative emotions, such as frustration, anger, irritability, sadness, anxiousness, indecisiveness, and feeling trapped. No wonder you're unhappy. Who wouldn't feel bad after saying these same things to themselves?

Negative emotions also prompt unpleasant physical responses, such as feeling tired, having an upset stomach or a headache, getting choked up, feeling like you're going to cry, or being unable to sleep. Because of the gears turning in your head, you may have difficulty concentrating. You may engage in mindless eating.

We feel something is wrong, but think there's nothing we can do about it. We feel stuck and give up, silently ashamed of ourselves. At this point, it's easy to disconnect from our true selves, our purpose. It's easy to give up on pursuing personal satisfaction and authentic happiness. We feel disconnected, because we *are* disconnected.

With heightened awareness, you'll start to see that there's a story, a string of disempowering sentences, you are believing to be true. Now that you know the power of these words, it's time to ask for help so you can turn the situation around. So how do you turn "I'm powerless" into "I'm powerful"? We are going to learn to direct our focus. We can hone in on positive thoughts that will generate happiness, rather than wallowing in negative self-talk, blaming, or justifying.

Let's look at Sally's story and what we may tell ourselves when feeling overwhelmed: *I have to get this project done. I never have the help I need. No one is competent or dependable.* Have you said this or something similar? Truth be told, we're capable of much harsher grievances. This version is pretty clean. Maybe you haven't said it out loud, but have you thought it?

Can you feel the perceived helplessness and blame in that statement? These words don't generate happiness or empowerment, do they? Take a moment and make these statements quietly to yourself and notice how you feel. Can you feel happy saying and believing this to be true? Yet, we talk this way to ourselves all the time, every day, unconsciously—and then wonder why we are unhappy in our lives. So, what can you say instead? Can you change the language and turn the feelings of powerlessness into feelings of power, thereby creating options?

This is the "renovation" process I mentioned earlier. It is the practice of directing your attention and focus by consciously choosing your words so you generate positive, happy thoughts, not negative rumination. When you apply the approach of creating change versus reacting, you prevent your mind from lazily defaulting to fault-finding and blame.

A renovation invites your mind to have a different experience of life and create different, more empowering options. This is a foundational tool for generating your own happiness. Learning to turn around negative thoughts is how we increase our level of happiness, direct our outcomes, and become self-responsible and empowered. What you focus on grows. Directing your focus to the positive and using uplifting language is a simple process that will change your life and generate more happiness.

Let's look at a sampling of Sally's negative, powerless statements again. Notice the disempowering language that creates a sense of helplessness:

- "**I have to** get this project done."

- "I **never** have the help **I need**."
- "**No one** is competent or dependable."

These words offer no choice, no way to triumph. That's not fun, is it? Take note of the language used and how it makes you feel. Now, let's learn, step-by-step, how to turn your self-talk around.

STEP ONE:
ASK, "WHAT AM I SAYING TO MYSELF?"

Do a quick reality check. Ask yourself if what you're saying to yourself and feeling is unquestionably true. Could there be another perspective? Do you really "have to"? What would happen if you didn't? Would you die? Is it absolutely true that you "never" have any help? Do you "need" help, or do you "want" help? Is absolutely "no one" competent or dependable?

STEP TWO:
INTRODUCE POSSIBILITY FOR CHANGE.

Begin with "it seems like" and recite the sentences again:

- "It seems like I have to get this project done."
- "It seems like I never have the help I need."
- "It seems like no one is competent or dependable."

Don't stop here. This is your opportunity to dump all your complaints and get unstuck. I've done this work many times and can still fill two pages. You may hear yourself say something like, "It doesn't just seem like it, it's true." Trust the exercise and keep going.

Notice how the meaning and sense of permanence changes with your choice of words. When you tell yourself, "It seems like", you are saying it could possibly be another way. When you question the truth of what you're saying, you create the possibility that reality could be other than how it seems in the moment.

Changing the language shifts the perceived permanence and dissolves the feelings of "stuckness", doesn't it? It's not so matter-of-fact anymore, is it?

STEP THREE:
OMIT DISEMPOWERING LANGUAGE.

Replace or remove limiting language, such as the following words and phrases:

- "I have to"
- "never"
- "no one"

STEP FOUR:
IDENTIFY INTENTION.

Ask yourself what you want to happen and what's important to you. So often we know what we *don't* want, but fail to identify what we *do* want (stated in positive language). Remember that it's acceptable to acknowledge yourself and your desires.

Could the following statements more accurately express what you mean?

- "I want to get this done."
- "It seems like I don't have help, but that's not necessarily true."
- "I've completed a good portion of the project and could use some help to relieve my stress."
- "Maybe I could find someone competent and dependable to help."

Modifying just a few of your words creates the possibility for change and gives you power. Notice how you feel with this more empowering vocabulary.

STEP FIVE:
MAKE A NEW DECLARATION.

Now that you've broken the negative thoughts and feelings, you can rephrase and recreate something even more powerful. I like using the word "actually" to signify that I am changing my mind and beginning anew:

- "Actually, I am committed to getting this project done with excellence."
- "How can I actually pull this off?"
- "I know the perfect person to help! They are amazing. I'm going to actually delegate part of this project and have it in my hands complete by end of day tomorrow."

This is your opportunity to generate happiness and build momentum by implementing key success principles. Give your word and produce something specific and measurable. Completing something challenging is satisfying and motivating. It takes a push to start from a standstill, but is much easier once you have some movement.

Learning to generate your own happiness doesn't mean you'll never get triggered and upset. For those times when you get really caught up in negativity or a stressful situation, it may be best to exercise self-acceptance rather than trying to force a renovation.

Here's another opportunity to try the approach introduced in Chapter Five to release negativity and affirm unconditional love: Take a deep breath. Notice how you feel. Rather than resist, let go and allow yourself to be compassionate. Surrender to what you're feeling that instant. Then, take another deep cleansing breath. Inhale through your nose, hold it for a moment, and exhale out your mouth. Say, "Even though I feel _____ (fill in the blank by acknowledging your emotions and physical sensations in your body), I completely and unconditionally love, appreciate, and accept myself." Repeat as needed.

The above statement may seem a little goofy at first, especially if you're not accustomed to acknowledging your feelings and practicing self-love and self-acceptance. That's okay. However, it's amazing how quickly this exercise can shift your perceived experience and reverse the negative message in your mind when facing something upsetting. Taking a moment to breathe and acknowledge will help you realize that, even though whatever you're dealing with may seem bad for you in the moment, you're most likely just reacting to a trigger. This process will help you clear your head and bring you back to the present, where you can then choose to generate a more empowering experience.

As mentioned previously, the language "Even though . . . I completely and unconditionally love, appreciate, and accept myself" used in the recommended approach above is similar to that used in EFT "tapping," this approach is not the full Emotional Freedom Technique. If interested, there are a number of books on the market explaining the principles and techniques of EFT and clinical EFT certified practitioners employing EFT Tapping.

A crucial part of generating your own happiness is changing or releasing debilitating negativity by taking notice of what you're saying and how it affects you. Ask yourself what you really want and then choose to say something powerful that supports that aim. Doing a mental renovation allows you to focus on what you want, versus getting stuck in what you don't want. Asking yourself the "right" questions can also make all the difference in getting to what you want. If you ask yourself, "Why me?", you will get an answer. However, this answer will focus on negative, external factors; it won't propel you forward. It tells your subconscious mind to identify circumstances to further support the limiting belief that you are stuck and things are beyond your control.

Instead of "why", ask "what" and "how" questions. Your subconscious mind will then help you come up with solutions. Asking yourself *what* and *how* will trigger your brain to look for opportunities and allow you to turn things around:

- *What feeds my soul?*
- *What can I learn from this experience?*
- *What do I really want?*
- *How can I get one step closer to my desired end result?*
- *What would the person I most admire do?*
- *What resources do I have available that I haven't used or considered?*

I also recommend shifting your physical state, your body language. Don't just tell yourself to shake it off; get up and do it. Get up and shake it off. Most people know that exercise can significantly improve your mood. Well, so can improving your posture.

I once saw a picture of Oprah Winfrey, sitting back in her chair with her hands behind her head. I could feel in my own body the satisfaction, confidence, and comfort I imagined she had in that instant. Compare that feeling to the feelings of disappointment and discouragement associated with your shoulders rounded and chin down. Simply changing your posture can be empowering and will send a completely different message to your brain.

Your physical state also impacts how others perceive and respond to you. For example, studies have shown a thirty-seven percent increase in sales by improving nonverbal communication. Having a happy facial expression and good posture creates a feeling of confidence and likeability in others when they engage with you.

You may or may not crave risk and adventure, but I prefer to throw my hands up in the air and scream when I ride a roller coaster. For me, it adds to the thrill and enjoyment, even if I'm faking it a little at first. If you're feeling stagnated and unsatisfied, try throwing your hands up in the air. I'm being serious—even if you're sitting at your desk and it seems silly. Would you rather feel silly or discouraged? Throw your hands up in the air once in a while and notice how you feel.

My suggested approaches are adaptations from a variety of methods I have used and continue to practice, based on what I have found to be most effective. Landmark Worldwide uses what they call "upgrading conversations" and "seemings" collages in their advanced Wisdom Courses (among many other distinctions and exercises). Their artistic practice of using collaging is freeing and complaints seem to disappear. The phrasing I suggest in the self-acceptance approach above is similar to that used in Emotional Freedom Techniques (EFT) as I've mentioned previously. EFT includes tapping on meridian points and has been reported to be effective at treating a variety of emotional, health and performance issues. You can find information about EFT in books and in videos.

Releasing blocks and letting go of limiting beliefs is an essential part of generating your own happiness and it is an ongoing practice. There are many other beneficial ways to relieve stress, emotional blocks and quiet a busy mind. For example, my go-to for times when my mind is busy working through the night is guided meditation. I believe the "right" method is the one you'll actually do. The only way to know if a method works for you is to put it to practice. Remember, you don't need to face your demons alone.

LET'S PLAY:

- PAY EXTRA ATTENTION TO YOUR VOCABULARY AND HOW WORDS MAKE YOU FEEL. PRACTICE OMITTING LIMITING PHRASES LIKE THE FOLLOWING ONES:

    - I HAVE TO

    - I NEED

    - I CAN'T

    - I DON'T KNOW HOW

- EXPERIMENT WITH MODIFYING BOTH YOUR VOCABU-LARY AND YOUR POSTURE AND NOTICE HOW YOU FEEL.

- DOWNLOAD YOUR "MENTAL RENOVATION" WORKSHEET FROM WWW.GENERATINGYOUROWNHAPPINESS.COM.

CHAPTER 13

SALLY COMES CLEAN
AND GETS REAL

SALLY HAS BEEN NUMBING her unhappiness for so long it has taken a toll on different areas of her life, including her finances, relationships, and health. She's been avoiding coming to terms with the root of her unhappiness.

Instead, Sally has made a habit of turning to mind-numbing and feel-good comforts, such as eating, drinking, and shopping, to temporarily sooth her overall dissatisfaction. It's not at all uncommon for Sally to end a long day falling asleep on the couch in front of the television.

Instead of waking up each morning feeling rejuvenated and nurturing her body with a healthy breakfast, Sally pushes the snooze button on her alarm until she knows she'll be hard-pressed to make it to the office on time.

She skips breakfast and picks up a coffee at the drive-through in an attempt to mask the tired hopelessness that permeates her being.

Even though she knows breakfast is the most important meal of the day, she intentionally opts for going without a meal as a strategy to keep her weight down. She also uses skipping breakfast to justify her afternoon Frappuccino when she needs a second pick-me-up. The problem is, the coffee doesn't perk her up or create a sense of satisfaction like it once did, not even with the sinful addition of chocolate or caramel syrup. Instead, she resents herself for giving in to the temptation and spending the money.

Sally hasn't admitted it to anyone—because she doesn't like the idea of taking medications unless they are absolutely necessary—but she is contemplating talking to her doctor about trying an antidepressant. She's worried her lack of motivation could be a sign of a more serious issue with depression or a hormonal imbalance. She has taken Benadryl the last couple of nights as a sleep aid, but she doesn't know how safe it really is.

Like Sally, so many people in our western culture live in a state of imbalance. Yet, we get used to it and hardly notice its destructive nature.

Even so, Sally's attempt to numb her pain hasn't worked. Instead, it has produced the habit of self-loathing and lowered her self-esteem around her body image. It's made her life circumstances seem worse. Blaming others and doing everything in her power to always be "right" certainly hasn't made her situation any better either—it has only put more strain on her relationships.

Do any of Sally's unhealthy habits sound familiar? Have you ever attempted to numb the pain (like drinking a few glasses of wine after losing your patience with someone at work or finishing off a bag of chips to alleviate stress) only to create more regret? Instead of helping you cope with the original disappointment, you now have both the original upset and the added guilt and shame of your numbing activity.

In my many years of working with people, I've seen this play out numerous times. We want a quick fix to our problems. We want to feel better without having to clean up all the disorder. So, we create distractions to avoid addressing the root cause of our unhappiness. Doing so, we fear, would be too painful or difficult.

Some have developed a pattern of seeking happiness through self-improvement. So often, we misidentify financial, physical, or emotional self-improvement as the solution we need. This is why the self-improvement industry pulls in more than ten billion dollars per year, with everything from fad diets to programs designed to help you build wealth. People tend to think improving their physical appearance or reaching some level of success will change their overall outlook on life. I have also found that people tend to look for a simple, one-size-fits-all, step-by-step approach to solving problems. They give more credibility to a "guru" than they do to themselves.

Many personal development consumers are repeat customers, but, sadly, are still unfulfilled. Studies show that the same person who purchases a self-help book or registers for a seminar made one or more similar purchases within the last year. However, these same consumers may fail to look within, so they waste time pursuing goals that don't truly resonate with them.

Here I am, an author in the "self-help" industry, and here you are reading this book. I enjoy a range of self-improvement topics myself and have spent my share of money in the industry. It satisfies my desire to learn something new. I love being introduced to new ideas and perspectives, and they get my creative gears turning.

I also work one-on-one with a coach because I've learned that I thrive when I have the right person supporting me, someone to shed light on a blind spot, show me a different perspective, or help me push through my own limiting beliefs. I still second-guess myself, but I'm able to work through my self-imposed limitations, which is extremely rewarding. I've learned that having the right structure, accountability, and personal support is essential for both my personal success and long-term happiness.

The fact is, however, if you are unwilling to look within, you can't expect reading self-help books to make your problems to magically disappear. And, if you don't learn to discover what generates genuine happiness for you and honor what speaks to your heart (versus following someone else's set of instructions), you can't expect to be happy.

If you get sold on or put your trust in something that doesn't resonate with you, it will ultimately lead to unhappiness. It may even keep you from dealing with unfinished business. In short, consuming any and every self-help tactic can sidetrack you, enticing you to put your energy into something not genuinely aligned with your happiness. This will have the same effect as procrastinating and hiding. You feel you are being productive, but you are deceiving yourself.

I believe most people are afraid of doing the "work" to generate authentic happiness because they think it's too hard. They may fear reliving painful experiences, or they may be afraid of failing. Sure, I've shed a few tears along the way to generating my own happiness, but mostly happy tears as a result of discovering something tender and beautiful within me.

In fact, it's the resistance to accepting things as they are that causes unhappiness. The process of letting go of the underlying limiting beliefs and allowing your greatness to shine is actually pretty easy and extremely rewarding.

Do you feel a stirring in your soul to move forward? Sally does. She knows it's time for her to get real and come clean.

Sally knows what has been haunting her and keeping her up at night, but still can't quite figure out how to turn it all around on her own. It would be helpful if Sally had a coach to support her and shed light on her journey, but she hasn't yet considered her own personal development a worthy investment. Fortunately for Sally, she's motivated by the pain she's been experiencing and knows it's time to do something about it. Once she gets going, she may even realize what she has been avoiding isn't as scary as it seemed.

Sally is buried in credit card debt, yet she has avoided admitting it—to herself or others. Buying things has kept her distracted from work and personal stress, but giving in to spending ultimately makes her ashamed. She tells herself she's irresponsible, and the guilt builds up. The truth is that Sally needs support, yet she's reluctant to admit she's been struggling emotionally or financially.

To make matters worse, she's angry with herself because she had planned to pay off her credit card debt with her annual bonus and tax return. Now, with the extra spending she has done the past few weeks, she knows she won't be able to pay it off, even though she's been afraid to look at the sum total of what she owes.

Breaking your word, even if to yourself, is a big deal. If you can't trust yourself, who can you trust? The impact of not keeping your word builds self-doubt, impedes your ability to have faith in yourself, and erodes your self-esteem.

Sally knows how to manage her finances and has helped dig her family out of debt before, so carrying this debt has been eating away at her. She tells herself she should know better. She's been procrastinating on coming up with a game plan. She hasn't asked for help because she's embarrassed. After all, she has created an image of herself that says she should be able to do everything on her own.

Many people feel pressured to hide the things they are ashamed of and often underestimate the damage self-criticism and suppressed shame can create. This kind of stress impacts the endocrine, lymphatic, and immune systems, making you vulnerable to disease, including autoimmune disease, cancer, heart disease, and more. How often do we underestimate the impact of our emotional well-being on our body?

Likewise, people tend to underestimate the value in coming clean and being honest about emotions and problems. Being authentic is a form of self-compassion; it frees you to be your best self. Being honest also invites others to be honest with you, which fosters loving relationships and deep connection. Restoring relationships and keeping your word builds trust, confidence, and true esteem. Honoring your word is extremely powerful.

Sally has also been anxious because she thinks her siblings want to have a meeting with her about her mom's living situation. She's been hiding and has intentionally let a couple of calls go to voice mail. She knows there are questions about her mother's monthly income and whether it will be enough to cover the care she'll need as her Alzheimers progresses.

Sally's sister has been looking at senior care facilities, and Sally's sister only considers the best of the best, especially when she's spending someone else's money. Sally's brother isn't in a position to help at all. In fact, she wonders if his living situation will come up when they talk, since he's been living in Mom's basement. Needless to say, Sally is not looking forward to meeting up with her brother and sister because she's afraid they will ask her for money, and she doesn't want any confrontation.

Sally has already been buying Mom's medication, running her errands, and cleaning her house once a week. Now, she's expecting her siblings will be asking her to supplement Mom's limited income so she can live in an assisted living center. Sally has always been the go-to in the family and has yet to say no. She has been hiding her debt, and it's causing her stress that her sibling are making false assumptions about her ability to help monetarily.

Sally has been upholding the image that she has everything together. People seem to either look up to Sally or envy her, but she knows she can't maintain this image much longer. She's going to have to come clean, not just with her family but, more importantly, with herself.

Sally had plans to take an important client to a big fundraiser. She had already purchased the tickets, which were not cheap, but knew she would also be expected to bid at the auction. Buying an expensive item she doesn't like or want was the last thing she needed. She called a friend she knew would appreciate the opportunity to attend the event and asked her to accompany her client.

That evening, she sat down with paper and pencil and started journaling, using step two of the renovation process. Her situation seemed hopeless, but she did it anyway, in the hope it would help alleviate her general frustration:

- It seems like I'm buried in debt.
- It seems like I did it to myself.
- It seems like everyone in my family takes advantage of me.
- It seems like my brother is a mooch.
- It seems like I don't have time to deal with this stuff.

She went on and on, dumping onto paper all the stuff she had been complaining about until there was nothing else. She felt a little relieved.

She asked herself, *If this wasn't real, if I didn't have all of these problems, what then?* She drew a blank. She knew what she didn't want in her life, but other than ending her suffering (which she knew she had inflicted on herself), she didn't really know what she wanted. She didn't know how to generate her own happiness. She wanted to trade frustration and disappointment for her old pep, but how?

Sally made the decision to face reality, clean up the mess, engage support, and create accountability for herself. For the first time in a long time, she was starting to feel motivated. She sat down in front of her computer and found a template for both a personal financial statement and a monthly budget. She pulled up statements of her accounts and started plugging in numbers. She was relieved and a bit surprised to see it wasn't as bad as she had thought, even though it was true that her bonus and tax return would not be enough to bail her out of debt.

Once Sally sat down and looked at what she was actually dealing with, she could see some obvious areas to cut spending, but what brought the greatest sense of satisfaction was doing the work. Purposefully engaging the problem allowed her to feel like she was regaining control. She was enjoying the experience of being in the driver's seat of her life, versus feeling like she was being towed down a bumpy road.

When Sally finally chose to come clean, she could clearly see the problems:

- She had been attending expensive fundraisers and supporting the children's hospital by bidding on silent auction items, yet she was only serving on the board because she hadn't recruited anyone to fill her shoes.

- She was a member of a networking association and paying monthly dues, but she hadn't attended a meeting in months, nor had she communicated with anyone in her group and now participating seemed awkward. The same was true for her gym membership.

- She had committed to pricey summer camps for her son, mostly out of peer pressure from other parents.

She was ready to start taking action, changing these easily identifiable strains on her income. She was also ready to come clean and be real in other areas of her life, beyond the debt. She picked up her phone and dialed her sister to schedule a family meeting. Normally Sally would cross her fingers, hoping to go straight to her sister's voice mail. Today was different, and, sure enough, her sister answered after the first ring.

The first thing her sister said was, "I was just thinking about you." Sally responded, "Really? Well, I was just thinking about you, too. In fact, I've been thinking about you and Mom's situation a lot and letting it make me crazy." Her sister chuckled and responded, "I know what you mean. I'm curious to hear your thoughts." Sally was a little amazed. She wouldn't have thought her sister cared at all about what she thought.

Sally said, "Well . . . to be honest, before we talk about a plan for Mom, I want to talk about what I've been dealing with and I want you to know I appreciate that you've been doing some legwork to explore assisted care options for Mom."

Sally could tell her sister was listening attentively. She took a deep breath and shared how she had been avoiding having this conversation out of fear that she would be expected to foot the bill for Mom and they would get into an argument. Sally went on to explain she was angry with herself for getting into debt and letting stuff go. She knew she didn't need to go into details. This was more than she'd ever shared with her sister about her personal life and knew the impact these few disclosures would have.

Sally's sister, with compassion in her voice, said, "You've always been the responsible, go-to person in the family. I hope you don't feel like we've taken you for granted. You know you can say no, right?" When there was no answer, Sally's sister repeated herself, "Right? And you know I'm here if you ever really get in a bind, right?"

Sally, for the first time in years, accepted the acknowledgement her sister was trying to make. In her mind, she questioned the validity of her sister's offer to help, but felt supported nonetheless. She ended the conversation with her sister by putting the date for a casual get-together on her calendar. Sally thought to herself, *That went better than I ever could have imagined.*

LET'S PLAY:

- IS THERE AN AREA OF YOUR LIFE IN WHICH YOU HAVE REFUSED TO COME CLEAN, FEARING WHAT OTHERS MAY THINK OR FEARING WHAT YOU WILL THINK OF YOURSELF IF YOU DRAG THE TRUTH INTO THE LIGHT?

- HOW WOULD IT FEEL TO EXPERIENCE THE FREEDOM SALLY FINDS IN BEING HONEST AND COMING CLEAN?

CHAPTER 14

YOUR TURN TO GET REAL

IT'S AMAZING HOW WE get paralyzed by fear of something completely imagined, immobilized by whatever prediction or assessment we've embraced. The simplest way to stop is to get out of your head and get into communication with others.

Unless we practice being self-responsible, saying what we authentically feel, we get caught up in the noise of our thoughts, believing what we're saying to ourselves. Most often, our thoughts are not truthful. Instead, they are triggered emotional responses to something that happened long ago. Everyone has experienced some form of disappointment and the resulting feelings of not being enough and/or not belonging. It's easy to live as though we are the only one who has been hurt and view the people in our lives as perpetrators of some sort.

Having power to generate your own happiness begins with being present with what is. I know it sounds cliché, but this is how "the truth sets you free." If you have loose ends and unfinished business in any area of your life, it will haunt you. It can be something as simple as forgetting to send a thank-you note. Annoyance over your omission can grow into self-criticism, eventually leading you to avoid interaction with the intended recipient. It's a downward spiral into unhappiness.

Neglecting any one area of our life affects everything, especially how you relate to yourself. At the end of the day, all we have is our word. When you dishonor your word by breaking promises, procrastinating, or avoiding, you dishonor yourself. If you can't have faith and trust in yourself, then you can't expect others to either.

It's time to get real with what is and start cleaning things up. Now, don't misinterpret me and feel like you're being punished or, worse, punish yourself. There's nothing "wrong" here (which we'll discuss later). Rather, getting real allows you to recognize opportunities. I like to think of this process as doing a personal SWOT analysis. If you're not familiar with the term "SWOT'" it's an acronym for identifying strengths, weaknesses, opportunities, and threats.

Now, don't worry. The getting-real process includes the strengths portion of the SWOT analysis and delivers opportunities. Let's reflect briefly on Sally's experience of getting real with her financial situation. When she took on being courageous and looked at what she was dealing with, her strengths shone.

Sally enjoys getting things organized. And, Sally is a doer. She likes to think of herself as a "get-it-doner." In fact, she wants the driven part of herself to become enlivened, and that's exactly what happened when she took the initiative to face the debt and make a plan. She's also one sharp cookie. She's not only intelligent and capable, but she also enjoys learning and being mentally (and physically, for that matter) challenged.

This chapter is about getting real and coming clean, so that means it's time for you, like Sally, to get to work—but only if you're committed to generating your own happiness. You don't *have to* do the work. It's a choice, as is the choice to generate happiness or unhappiness.

The "getting real" portion means being honest about what you're telling yourself and what you're really dealing with. If you don't know where you are, you can't design a map to where you want to go.

Start with scanning the different areas of your life. Where are you feeling constrained or stuck? What actions can be taken to clean stuff up? Who do you need to talk to? What can be done to create some freedom in the areas that are out of balance?

I recommend taking a look at each of the following areas:

- Work
- Relationships
- Money/finances
- Health
- Spirituality
- Growth
- Community service

You can begin by scoring each area of your life on a scale of one to ten, with one representing complete dissatisfaction in that area and ten representing bliss in that area. The areas of discontentment indicate a lack of harmony; something is out of balance, and you have work to do to restore integrity. These are opportunities for growth and development. Woo-hoo!

Now that you've identified areas of dissatisfaction, or come to terms with what is, what opportunities do you see? What speaks to you or stands out? For example, is there a strained relationship or guilt about something you've said? Or maybe you broke a promise, but you never acknowledged it or communicated your new intention. Have you been longing for a relationship, but haven't taken any action toward fulfilling your true desire? Are you relating to Sally's financial circumstances? Perhaps you could benefit from a plan of action to reduce debt and build wealth.

I can't encourage you enough to pick one or more opportunities, big or small, and take action toward creating harmony in that area. My wish is that you take this on and make an intentional effort to enjoy the process and satisfaction of cleaning up these areas in your life.

To this day, when I find myself stressed, I can create a sense of calm and satisfaction by organizing a drawer or closet, tending to my garden, or reconciling my accounting records. That's right. I find joy in "bean counting", and it's a beautiful thing. You may enjoy these tasks as well, or you may find joy in asking someone to help you with tasks you don't enjoy. Either style is great. Just do it and enjoy.

If you happen to have everything in your life in order, yet you're not quite satisfied, consider whether you've been playing it safe or letting fear of failure limit you. Maybe the best formula for you isn't confessing and cleaning up. Maybe stepping out of your comfort zone and challenging your performance fears is your next step. If just the idea of risking and failing makes you a little squirmy or anxious, you're likely empowering a negative belief in that area. It may be time to challenge yourself to come up with a big, hairy, audacious goal, something you're afraid you may not be able to accomplish.

I'm challenging you to look within and identify what speaks to your soul. Often, there's a longing to achieve greatness, but there's no rush to step into the unknown. There's a point where some people need to get more organized, and there's a point where the super organized need to be stretched beyond their comfort level. If you identify with the latter, I suggest challenging yourself to take on something that makes you a bit uneasy. Challenge the thought, "What if I can't deliver?" Step out into the unknown and pursue greatness.

LET'S PLAY:

- WHAT HAVE YOU BEEN HIDING OR UNWILLING TO ADDRESS IN YOUR LIFE THAT YOU KNOW IS HOLDING YOU BACK IN SOME WAY?

- HOW CAN YOU COME TO TERMS WITH WHAT'S SO AND EMPOWER YOURSELF?

- TAKE ADVANTAGE OF THE RESOURCES AT WWW.GENERATINGYOUROWNHAPPINESS.COM BY UTILIZING THE SELF-ASSESSMENT WORKSHEET TO TAKE PERSONAL INVENTORY.

CHAPTER 15

RESTORING INTEGRITY

WE HAVE BEEN EXAMINING our beliefs to understand ourselves more deeply and looking at areas of life where we can be self-responsible and take action to generate or direct our own happiness. We have been noticing how automatic reactions to preexisting, negative beliefs and associations can sabotage our happiness. Most often, this process happens without our being aware. Doubt, stress, and worry are part of the human condition, but now we're starting to take notice.

We have mentioned being "mindful", but it's time to unpack this term. Practicing mindfulness is attentively observing your thoughts and feelings in the present moment, without judging, without automatically evaluating them as right or wrong. By actively practicing mindfulness, you are able to shift your perspective and, in turn, your experience of the moment.

Generating your own happiness is possible when you realize you are the source of your life. In other words, you have power, in each and every moment, to determine your mindset and experience. Life is not merely the result of external circumstances, something that happens to you. However, we often forget our role and do not apply our power, allowing life to drag us along.

Think about how easily life becomes routine and how often you find yourself simply going through the motions, without deliberate thought. Think also of the difficult circumstances and hardships we face; we feel truly limited, so we believe we are at the mercy of the universe. In these moments, mindfully taking notice of our humanity may be the best option.

Happiness is not a product of everything in life being exactly as we wish. Even though we seem to derive happiness from our external experiences, happiness is a state of being that arises from *within us*—a state of being we can call forth. Mindfulness is a part of that.

We can see from Sally's experience how one might become detached from their own feelings or needs. Sally often sacrificed her own happiness, attempting to do what was "right", rather than listening to her own thoughts. Pleasing others—to the detriment of one's true fulfillment—might include portraying an image or fulfilling expectations based on societal rules and standards.

Sally put a lot of energy into avoiding the judgment of others, while "shoulding" herself, day in and day out, detached from her personal needs. She found herself stuck in a rut, feeling resentful and obligated to maintain the life she had built for herself. Ultimately, Sally lost sight of what was right for her, what could feed her soul. She was disconnected and out of touch with what spoke to her on a deep level and thus lacked a compelling reason to live. She wasn't clinically depressed, but she was disconnected from her own tenderness, magnificence, and individuality.

After reading Sally's story, it's time for you to practice mindfulness and call forth your most magnificent self. It's time to walk in authenticity by generating your own happiness. Remember, happiness is our true essence, and unhappiness is a sign that we are being untrue to ourselves. Unhappiness is a state of turmoil in which we react to the environment, versus using discernment—keen insight and intuitive understanding—to respond to life.

Notice how Sally experienced a renewed sense of life when she started using discernment to question what she was saying to herself. She got out of her head, shut down the "shoulds", and leaped into action. She dared to have authentic communication with the people in her life, and she dared to look within. In short, Sally experienced authentic happiness when she restored her integrity.

We commonly associate integrity with rules, with maintaining a moral uprightness. However, this definition doesn't properly express how powerful integrity really is. Living with integrity is more than avoiding doing something "wrong." Yes, ethically speaking, integrity encompasses honesty and truthfulness, but we are seldom taught that, first and foremost, integrity is being honest and truthful with yourself. Shakespeare said, "To thine own self be true." He understood the power of being honest and truthful with yourself first. Only then can you be truly honest with and help others.

The word "integrity" is derived from the Latin word *integer*, meaning whole and complete. In this context, integrity is an inner sense of wholeness, which comes from living honestly, in harmony with your core values. I like to think of living in integrity as living a life consistent with your highest values and aspirations, being true to yourself, and striving for the highest good. Sometimes we neglect to include ourselves in this equation. We can mistakenly think that fulfilling a deep longing is somehow selfish and forget we are part of the highest good.

Integrity isn't something you learn. Integrity is something you faithfully listen to and honor. Integrity is doing what is right—not for attention, accolades, rewards, or fear of doing something wrong—simply because it is the right thing to do.

Landmark Education defines integrity as being whole and complete by honoring your word and doing what you said you would do when you said you would do it. When you don't live by this standard, you must acknowledge the negative impact and recommit to living in accordance with integrity. When you do, life is noticeably more workable. This kind of inner harmony is the foundation for power and effectiveness in your life. You are empowered and decisive when you honor your word.

When you dishonor your word by breaking promises, procrastinating, avoiding, or resisting, you are, in turn, dishonoring yourself. We naturally think about keeping our word to earn the respect and trust of others, yet we discount how we undermine our relationship to ourselves when we are not living the truth.

Honoring your word is a form of self-honor. The more you practice making and keeping promises that are in alignment with what's genuinely important to you, the more you learn to have faith and trust in yourself. Restoring integrity builds genuine self-esteem. It gives you the confidence to manifest a meaningful life and is, perhaps, the most essential practice in generating your own happiness.

Examine an area of your life in which you feel stuck. Ask yourself, *What am I saying or believing that leaves me feeling disempowered?* I'm willing to bet, underneath your unhappiness is an issue with integrity or the resulting inauthenticity that comes from a lack of honesty. Remember, authenticity is the degree to which you are true to your personality, spirit, or character, despite external pressures.

Jean-Paul Sartre, a key figure in the philosophy of existentialism, called such inauthenticity "bad faith" (French, *mauvaise foi*). When human beings, under pressure from social expectations, adopt false values and disown their innate freedom of choice, it creates misalignment, a disconcerting feeling of "bad faith."

While I don't believe most people choose to act in bad faith—that is, they have no evil intention to cause harm—I do believe most people can relate to feeling like they are at the mercy of external circumstances. When caught in a sticky situation, we commonly compromise our integrity to avoid criticism. We fear potential negative consequences or feel stress from external pressures. Thus, to avoid an unpleasant outcome or to fit in and be respected, we make a short-sighted, inauthentic choice. It's not wrong, it's human.

Ultimately, you can learn mindfulness techniques to recognize and overcome this common human reaction. Once mindfully aware of your inner truth, you can shift from a default response of dishonesty, choosing instead to keep inner harmony and act with integrity and wholeness.

Our "inner compass" is our deep sense of knowing and our feeling of purpose. Most have been taught to ignore this inner compass and use their analytical mind to make decisions. As a result, we are not as comfortable with honoring our intuition—we have learned to discount or discredit it. But your inner compass is a fundamental tool for living a life of meaning and purpose, which is filled with joy, inner peace, contentment, and fulfillment. In other words, our intuition is connected to our genuine happiness.

What happens when we turn off this inner compass? We feel out of balance because we are no longer living in harmony with our inner intelligence. Neglecting to honor yourself and abandoning this inner intelligence will inevitably lead to disorder and unhappiness.

Living in harmony with your inner compass begins with knowing where you stand and what's important to you. Without recognizing it, many people learn to follow the crowd and forfeit their personal integrity. They stop prioritizing what truly matters to them. When we do this, we are fragmented and eventually experience pain and unhappiness.

In contrast, when you honor your core values and your word and values are congruent with your external behaviors, you are living in integrity. You will inevitably experience peace and a sense of being complete.

Sally, rather than following what she knew deep down to be true, acted to gain acceptance and was motivated by self-preservation. Eventually, she became jaded, second-guessing herself and giving her power away. She was out of alignment with her true self and began to feel she didn't belong.

Since childhood, all she wanted was for everyone to get along and be happy, so the tendency to please others at the expense of her own desires is deep-seated. When Sally would notice lonely kids on the playground, she would try to include them at recess. She would even give up her favorite piece of candy or prized possession if she thought it could turn a frown into a smile. She was taught by her parents, teachers, and church to treat others as she would like to be treated. Though her love and compassion for others came naturally, she made it her job to always put others first.

Sally used to play on her street with her older brother and a few of the neighborhood kids. At the end of the block lived a grouchy older woman named Mabel. Whenever a ball or anything entered her yard, Mabel would confiscate it. One day, the idea was pitched by the bully of the group that they should jump over her wall and get their stuff back.

Sally knew it was a bad idea, but she didn't speak up. She ignored and dishonored her sense of right and wrong. When the kids saw Mabel's car pull away, they jumped the brick wall and entered her house through a window. Sally followed with hesitation, feeling the struggle between doing what she knew was the right thing to do and going along with the majority. She knew it was wrong, but she did it anyway because she didn't want to be judged or teased. She prioritized fitting in over honoring her discernment.

As adults in the workplace, this happens all the time. We learn to look the other way or give up something that's important to us because we're taught to value the boss, paycheck, or looking good over our own values and intuition. Often, people think they can't get what they want without manipulation, yet manipulation puts you at odds with integrity.

Next thing Sally knew, a few of the kids started ransacking the place. Sally got more and more nervous as she knew it would be obvious that they broke in. It was apparent they weren't simply looking for their balls and Frisbees. She ran home and watched for the other kids to come back, but before they did, Mabel returned. As Mabel opened her front door, Sally saw the other kids jump over the wall and scatter.

As it turns out, one of the neighbors had witnessed the kids entering the property and the police had already been called. Sally and a couple of the other kids had been identified. Even after being caught and punished, Sally never ratted out the mastermind of the group, but she spent the rest of the summer alone because the other kids shamed her for being afraid and leaving them.

That summer, Sally made the decision that she didn't belong and no one really cared about her. Deep down, she was upset with herself for not following her gut or standing up for what was right, but she never expressed those thoughts to anyone—nor did she consciously acknowledge them herself.

It was clear to her that she had gone along with the group when she knew doing so was wrong, but afterwards, they didn't have her back and judged her. From then on, she never fully trusted anyone. What wasn't clear to her was that the decisions she had made would be instilled in her subconscious and would come up in subtle ways for years to come. Sally was loyal to group-think versus her own discernment. Not only did Sally lose trust in others, she lost faith and trust in herself. She had compromised her integrity.

Like Sally, we give up our integrity to survive in the world and be accepted. It's much easier to not rock the boat. So, you have a cocktail, even when you don't feel like drinking, or you make an excuse when you don't want to accept an invitation, rather than decline. It's easier to give up on personal convictions than to step out in faith and be different. It's easier to protect your pride and pretend like you don't care that you are out of step with what is right, with your own sense of honesty.

Yet, compromising your personal integrity, by not honoring that which speaks to you, will inevitably impact every area of your life. In fact, any area of your life that's out of alignment will continue to disrupt your flow of happiness until you come clean, forgive yourself, and create a new possibility.

You may not see how you have blamed yourself or how you've compensated in response to former events, and that's okay. I don't believe it's necessary to rehash events from your past, but I do believe it's extremely helpful to practice mindfulness and then forgiveness. We will cover forgiveness and letting go in chapter eighteen. You may also want to refer back to chapter five, which discusses unconditional love.

Being in harmony with your inner compass means you are being consistent with your core values. You are honest and sincere, acting with compassion toward yourself. When you find yourself unhappy or discouraged, it's an indication you are out of inner alignment. If you are experiencing anger, frustration, resignation, or some other negative response, it stems from a limiting belief or some form of blame (your ego is holding on to being right about something).

This is an opportunity to identify inauthenticity and restore personal integrity. Again, this practice requires discernment. We all have learned behaviors, and if left to its own devices, the mind can justify anything. Remember, true discernment includes mindful insight without judgment.

Ask yourself the following questions:

- *Where am I unhappy (mad, sad, or afraid)?*
- *What am I saying to myself, pretending about, or avoiding?*
- *Where am I making excuses?*

If you're doing any of these things, it doesn't mean you are a bad person. Judging yourself as bad or wrong couldn't be further from the point— although we're all capable of going there. The ultimate consequence to integrity issues is unhappiness because you are dishonoring your word or disconnecting from your truth. There's either integrity *or* imbalance. The two states don't coexist.

Because most people are uncomfortable with imbalance and the accompanying negative emotions, they block the feeling, but there's a wonderful advantage if you allow yourself to feel the conflict. Your internal senses will tell you whether you're in integrity or out of balance. You'll know.

When you notice the imbalance, are you going to ignore it or acknowledge it? If you acknowledge it, you get to explore it further. If you explore the imbalance, you invite integrity in. It's an opportunity to be present with yourself and create alignment. It creates options. When you stop and pay attention, you can experience internal resonance and genuine fulfillment.

Until you invite integrity back in, you are inviting struggle. It happens in a nanosecond. You have the choice: buy into the idea that there's nothing you can do, or inquire within. Integrity allows you to be present with yourself. When you have authentic integrity, you can be truly happy.

When you are out of integrity, it's because you don't trust yourself and the divine. Could it be you are distrusting that your best and highest good will be answered? Could it be you are avoiding responsibility for all you could become?

LET'S PLAY:

- HOW CAN YOU PRACTICE MINDFULNESS EACH DAY? WHAT FEELINGS DO YOU NORMALLY JUDGE AS "BAD"?

- WHAT VALUES ARE IMPORTANT TO YOU PERSONALLY? WHAT ARE YOUR CORE VALUES?

- WHERE ARE YOU CURRENTLY USING YOUR ANALYTICAL MIND TO MAKE DECISIONS, RATHER THAN TRUSTING YOUR INNER COMPASS?

- DO YOU SENSE AN AREA OF IMBALANCE IN YOUR LIFE? IF SO, WHAT WILL YOU DO TO ADDRESS IT?

CHAPTER 16

HONORING YOUR CALLING

WHAT IF BELIEVING YOU are at the mercy of circumstance is really just a sexy excuse to avoid being self-responsible, to avoid taking a risk and putting your authentic self out front, where others can see you? How often do you default to playing it safe? What if you are missing your calling, the unique reason you were put on this earth at this time?

You may start to get crafty and manipulative because you want something, but don't trust the divine to serve your best and highest good. Where is your trust at this moment? What do you believe about your purpose and path? Whether you believe the divine is God, an angel, or a sixth sense, you can tap into this source to gain confidence and access your truth.

Sometimes the journey to your purpose will involve unpleasant emotions. Remember, being mindful means you feel *all* your feelings—even the "bad" ones—without judgment. In fact, when you allow yourself to feel a negative emotion, the sensation can lead you to unveil something inauthentic that has been holding you back. This is where discernment comes in, and you must listen to your higher self or god within.

Believe it or not, negative emotion is golden. Whenever you experience a loss of power in an area of your life, it's a clue there is some sort of inauthenticity, something you're not seeing for yourself or expressing freely and lovingly.

When Sally faced the discomfort over her mother's care and came clean with her sister, it was an opportunity to regain a connection with what was important to her. It deepened her relationship to her sister. If she'd bought the story she was telling herself, believing her sister was wrong and her circumstances were holding her back, she would have missed the opportunity to break through the mental turmoil, not to mention the opportunity to have a loving relationship with her immediate family.

What Sally had avoided dealing with for years took minutes to transform. What had seemed so significant wasn't. Imagine what else could be possible with a little courage and vulnerability.

Let me give an example from my own life of how I was able to benefit from feeling sadness when I chose to be true to myself. Prior to writing this book, I had created pretty significant change in my life. I had worked with a life coach and successfully met the man of my dreams, my husband. When I met him, I owned A19, a ceramic lighting manufacturing company, a Jazzercise fitness franchise, and Loft 204, an art gallery. I had also gone through a period of heightened, intuitive awareness and sensitivity, or what I call "woo woo"—but that's a story for another time.

I loved virtually every aspect of all three businesses, especially the people in each community. I enjoyed being at a stage in my life where I was openly sharing myself and experiencing a love of life. My life was pretty darn great, but I had a lot going on.

People told me I had too much on my plate, and if I was going to make marriage work, I had to let some stuff go. I kept hearing, "You can't do it all." While some days were a bit stressful as I ran from one gig to another, more often I felt like I was on cloud nine. I felt especially fortunate, but I had been single for a long while and was entering unfamiliar territory, becoming both a wife and stepparent, so I started second-guessing myself. Maybe other people saw something or knew something I didn't. This was where I abandoned faith and trust in myself and was guided instead by the opinions of others.

I considered scaling down and reducing my time commitments. Letting go of my lighting company didn't seem smart or feasible because it was my main source of income, and I felt obligated to my employees and their families.

Notice I said "obligated." I told myself to prioritize stability and the needs of others over touchy-feely personal fulfillment. Teaching aerobics and hosting art openings benefitted me personally, keeping me fit and social. They were fun, so it hardly occurred to me that they were a lot of work. I even enjoyed the business side of both—although the motivating force was never the money.

So, what did I do? A friend of mine took over the art gallery, and I decided to sell the fitness business. To be honest, my decision to sell my Jazzercise franchise was triggered by a knee-jerk reaction to feeling like I didn't have the support I needed. However, the decision came while listening to the opinions of others about what I should and shouldn't do as I got married. I justified my decision by convincing myself that I was no longer doing a good job and teaching Jazzercise was not worth the stress. Remember, this is the same commitment that previously contributed to my experience of being on cloud nine.

I would like to say that I have absolutely no regrets about decisions I've made in my life, but I was especially sad about giving up my fitness classes. The transition did not go as smoothly as I had hoped, yet I knew there was much to learn throughout the entire transition. After grieving the loss, I allowed myself to acknowledge the emotions and asked myself what it was about teaching that touched me so deeply. This is where I practiced what I preach. I sat with the unpleasant emotion of sadness and asked what it could teach me.

In a moment of contemplation and inquiry, asking for divine guidance, I had a vision of myself up on a stage with a microphone. I experienced a deep sense of knowing that I was on the stage because I had written a book.

A wave of fear rolled over me at the thought of writing a book. I'm pretty sure the words that instantly came to mind were, *Oh, crap.* (Okay. Maybe it was really the F-word.)

Next, a new business idea flooded my mind, and I was incredibly excited. I jumped up from where I was, grabbed my notebook, and jotted down notes as fast as I could. The next morning, I got to work, building support to bring my vision to fruition. The most valuable piece of this story is that I wasn't answering or responding to a logical challenge in my mind. I was listening to and honoring my feelings, which ultimately led me to the challenge of my soul. I was in touch with my inner compass, and I could see my calling, my next adventure.

I can attest to making plenty of "mistakes" in my life, as far as failing to produce a specific, desired result or to fully accomplish a goal, but I don't consider them failures. Any regret I may have is because I second-guessed myself, reacted to an emotional trigger, or attempted to follow someone else's advice or standards over my own. I have never, ever regretted putting trust in and following my sense of intuition, my values, or my calling.

Letting go and trusting your calling takes courage. Sharing about my own "woo woo" experiences in print certainly requires nerve. Yet, there's a difference between trusting yourself and the divine versus putting your trust in someone else or choosing a path simply because you want to end the suffering.

Here's an example: Sally's son wants something. She pulls out her credit card, even though her gut tells her no. She knows she shouldn't do this financially, and it's not really in his best interest either. Then she looks at little Timmy and wants him to have the excitement she sees in his eyes, so she buys it anyway.

Later it comes back up for her, and she hears herself say, *I shouldn't have given in.* She now regrets a decision she made to avoid feeling the pain of disappointing her son; it was not a decision made with discernment. These inner conflicts happen with decisions in every area of life, with relatives, friends, work, and self. Have you ever lost sleep because your mind was busy trying to make the "right" decision? Or, worse, have you ever been stuck in blame or justification mode, second-guessing yourself and full of inner turmoil?

Whether you have a good excuse or not, not taking an appropriate action eats away at self-esteem and siphons off your happiness—until you take ownership and restore your credibility (both internally and externally). Even if you have a really good excuse, you'll be left with justification, rather than what's important to you, what brings you true joy.

When you put your trust in a passion that speaks to you and give it your all, even if you fail at fully accomplishing it, you won't have regrets. There really is no such thing as being a failure when you are true to your inner guide.

Trying circumstances will come, and you will, at times, experience a loss of power. Even so, the real power comes through communicating with integrity and in honoring your word, even if it means revising your word and taking baby steps to reestablish your integrity. Having integrity requires being genuine about where you've been untrue.

Regardless of the impact, you must honor what's sincerely important to you. You may have to let go of the need to be right in order to say what's true for you. When you do, you can have faith that you are aligned with the greatest and highest good. When you share yourself authentically, people will resonate with your integrity and will give you their blessing to follow your way. The universe aligns with integrity.

But here's the thing about integrity. Even though much of our life has been dedicated to learning the rules of society, personal integrity isn't learned. I believe it's innate within us. We have a natural longing for goodness, compassion, beauty, connection, and truth, yet we've learned to protect ourselves from being vulnerable, and we've detached from the deeper passion within us.

We often relate to our core values through what we're taught is morally right and wrong, but when you learn to identify and honor your true core values, they provide guidance, direction, meaning, and a sense of purpose. It is this sense of direction, meaning, and purpose that leads you to genuine happiness. The Dali Lama said, "The purpose of our lives is to be happy."

It is my belief that you are being called to honor and manifest whatever it is (even if you can't put words to it) that speaks to you. You may feel drawn to make the world a better place and strive toward world peace. You may experience deep compassion and yearn to make a difference in the life of another. You may feel compelled to share your vulnerabilities or something else itching to come out. You may sense there's a form of art wanting to be expressed through you. You may feel the duty to lead your community in some capacity. You may be passionate about being a steward for the environment or all living things.

Your calling may seem unreachable or frightening, or it may seem miniscule. Whatever it is that speaks to you, whatever you choose, my wish is that you live true to yourself in full integrity and enjoy the happiness that living that way brings. You are worthy.

LET'S PLAY:

- PRACTICE HONORING YOUR WORD BY ONLY PROMISING TO DO WHAT YOU'RE GENUINELY COMMITTED TO.

- IF THERE IS A PROMISE YOU HAVE NOT FULFILLED OR AN EXPECTATION YOU DON'T PLAN TO MEET, COMMUNICATE IT. DO WHAT YOU SAY YOU WILL DO AND BE HONEST WHEN AN EXPECTATION OR REQUEST IS NOT IN ALIGNMENT WITH YOUR CALLING.

- WHAT IS YOUR CALLING IN THIS SEASON OF LIFE? IT MAY HELP TO FIRST IDENTIFY YOUR PASSIONS.

CHAPTER 17

WHAT IF?
A JOURNEY OF QUESTIONS

BEFORE WE DISCUSS FURTHER how to identify and honor your calling, I invite you to go with me on a self-questioning journey. I invite you to do your own gut check. In other words, don't just take my word for anything. Instead, see if any of what we're about to explore rings true for you or if you notice anything that stands out for you personally. I also invite you to play and let your imagination go free as you respond to my questions.

What if, in the game of life, all judgments, fear, and justifications are really just sexy excuses that keep you from playing big? What if they are roadblocks to keep you from venturing into the realm of the unknown and unfamiliar? What if the circumstances that leave you feeling powerless are keeping you from walking out onto the skinny branches and taking a risk?

What if risk is what stands between you and living a life that allows your greatness to be seen? And what if that which you are trying to avoid, fix, or change—that which seems blatantly wrong—contains the most valuable gifts of all?

So much of life is spent learning to be right and strategizing about how to do things correctly. We place a lot of emphasis and value on education and knowledge. Science sets out to prove or disprove. In school, we learn to identify the right answers, avoiding being wrong or making mistakes. We're being assessed from the time we're born, and we learn to assess others as well.

What is your earliest memory of being evaluated? Did you ever work really hard in preparation for a test and get a lower grade than you expected? Were you ever ashamed of yourself because you know you could have done better? Did you ever want a role in a play or a position on a team, but lost it to someone deemed better? When is the first time you felt like you didn't measure up in some capacity? As an adult, do you ever find yourself playing it safe because you think you aren't good enough, you don't want to fail, or you consider the risk too large? What do you consider risky? Is it failing? Do you fear potential loss? Do you ever panic at the thought of not knowing what to do next?

Did you know most people get stuck or are triggered around an under-lying belief of not being enough in one form or another, from a sense of not belonging or because they feel like they are all alone? We each have our own way of describing what we perceive and how it shows up in our lives, but our problems are not as unique as we sometimes think they are.

Who doesn't want to avoid making mistakes? Who doesn't want to be right and avoid being wrong? We put a lot of energy into being right, doing the right thing, and preventing certain scenarios. Many people even sacrifice love, connection, and companionship—basic wants—to avoid getting hurt. To some extent, we are all afraid of experiencing pain, of being rejected or humiliated. Do you have a unique fear or circumstance that holds you back?

What if focusing on these sexy excuses and difficult circumstances is keeping you from being responsible as the source of your own life? Remember, "responsible" refers to your ability to be responsive—verses reactive. It doesn't mean you are to blame. Rather, it refers to your power to cause, to give rise to, to create.

What if we really do have the power to create and cause everything in our lives? Or, what if there actually is a reason for everything that happens, other than the reasons our mind typically comes up with? And what if we are missing out because of our efforts to ensure our ego avoids challenge or discomfort? I'm not setting out to prove or disprove. I'm just inviting you to wonder with me: what if?

What if obstacles and challenges are meant to make the experience of life more exhilarating, like adventures you would design into a game or build into your travel itinerary? Or what if, just as you are about to step outside of the box or have a really big win, life throws you a major curveball to test your commitment? What if?

What if overcoming or pushing through these challenges is how our soul expands, how we get the most out of our experience of life? What if everything that stops us in life is a "sexy excuse" to keep us from getting out of our comfort zone and playing "full out" or being the big, bold, beautiful expression of our true self? And, what if fear is just another "sexy excuse", one so seductive that it seems real and justifiable, yet it only keeps you from taking action?

Now, don't get me wrong. I would never suggest you discount your fear of an innately dangerous situation. In fact, I hope you know to check in with your gut feeling or intuition and are wise. I'm also not suggesting that having fears is wrong or bad and needs to be fixed or overcome—remember, it's important to notice feelings instead of judging them. What I *am* suggesting is that you notice when fear comes up and use discernment, then choose how to respond to fear and other obstacles. Do you tend to dance with, step over, or surrender? There is no right or wrong answer. I simply want you to know you have choices.

How often have you let fear, in one form or another, stop you from taking an action or keep you from pursuing a goal or dream? What if diving head-first into the fear, discomfort, or unforeseen circumstance is actually a shortcut to unveiling what your heart and soul desire most? Are you willing to chance it?

Great! Then let's go. Let's move forward in learning how to generate true soul happiness.

USING A STREAM-OF-CONSCIOUSNESS STYLE OF WRITING, ASK YOURSELF YOUR OWN "WHAT IF" QUESTION AND ENJOY WHATEVER COMES UP.

CHAPTER 18

BEING HUMAN

ACTUALLY, I'M CONFIDENT THAT what you're looking to uncover isn't entirely new to you, but if you're like the rest of the human race (and Sally), you experience periods of forgetfulness. You become disconnected from what your soul wants most. So often, we get caught up in the hustle and bustle of life and the frenzied human tendency to pursue pleasure and avoid pain. When in this state, we're numb to the miracle of the present moment and what our soul is saying.

We tend to get caught up in nostalgia or judgment of the past and anticipation of, or anxiety over, the future. Think about how often these tendencies are used in sales and politics to control us or stir up an emotional reaction. All potential for true happiness and your power to create lies in the present moment within your soul. Access to your soul's desires can only exist in the present moment.

When we become the observer, we can see the madness in our thoughts and our need to assess everything. When you attempt to still the mind, you can observe how it races from one thought to the next.

Happiness is a quality or attribute of your soul and your inner spirit. Unhappiness exists when we compare our circumstances with a perceived "should be" state of the past, present, or future. Unhappiness is when we are not looking at the present moment or when we are arguing with "what is."

I say happiness is the experience of being in a generative state, honoring what speaks to your soul. It means listening to your inner voice and being free to choose your own path in life. It is creating a life consistent with your highest values and aspirations. We've talked about all of this before, yet it bears repeating.

I also want to warn you of a common pitfall. Most people get confused—and, therefore, don't have true happiness—because they don't understand *how* to be happy. In fact, thinking and believing, *I don't know how*, is probably the sexiest of my own excuses, the one capable of leaving me the most discouraged.

Fortunately, I have been developing the skill of discernment, and I'm not against asking for help, especially in the face of this limiting belief. That doesn't mean the fear of not knowing how to do something doesn't come up again and again throughout my life. Sometimes I catch it right away and take it on as a fun challenge, with a "game on" approach; at other times, I fall into its trap and have to climb out. *I don't know how* can seem very real.

As we discussed early on, people get confused about where happiness comes from. But you know better now and have the tools to go forward. We know that pleasures and comforts don't create happiness, nor does success (not to discount the joy of accomplishment). Happiness is a full-body experience: physical, emotional, and spiritual. True happiness is a quality of spirit. Happiness begins by knowing ourselves deeply. Generating a life that makes you happy starts with exploring yourself thoroughly, both your inner and outer uniqueness.

Sadly, most people don't want to explore. They prefer familiarity and predictability versus delving into the unknown or uncomfortable parts of life. Yet the thrill of the unknown and the joy of discovering deeper layers of ourselves is part of the happiness journey. If you want to thrive, you will have to be at peace with the unknown. It's inevitable. Like it or not, we are entering unchartered territory.

Because of the fear of the unknown, people use their minds to scan the world, to make sense of it so it's more predicable or familiar. When we think we understand what's happening, we feel safe; the familiar brings relief. Yet, we confuse the feeling of relief from our anxious worries for the feeling of happiness. Can you see how this is not happiness?

Because most people do not like living in the unknown, they often give up their happiness to live in some form of predictable structure and daily routine. They forfeit greater fulfillment for having control over their life. This is inside-the-box thinking. When you end up using your mind to create a safe, predictable, familiar daily routine, you are living inside the box, and that is not generating happiness. That is generating safety.

The soul is where happiness is generated. It is the part of you that desires something that, in the moment, may seem like an impossible request. It's that nudge deep within you that says, *Let's take a risk.*

Let me be clear: it's not the "risk", in and of itself, that makes the soul happy. Happiness comes in the action of honoring what speaks to you at the soul level, what I refer to as your inner compass.

Happiness is not the result of something happening *to* you or being given to you, though this is what we've been taught. For example, as an infant, any time you felt discomfort, someone typically gave you something to make you feel better. We don't actually learn what real happiness is when we're young. Instead, we learned that happiness is receiving something external that helps us feel better—whether it's a soothing object or a feeling, such as pleasing others. We're taught, *do a good job and don't disappoint, and you will receive rewards*—and then you're supposed to be happy. Unfortunately, we often get stuck thinking that happiness is dependent on someone else's intervention or reaction.

I have learned through experience to take notice and not only *allow* discomfort and emotion but also to *embrace* it and trust my feelings in the moment. Instead of trying to stuff emotions or numb pain and discomfort, I pay close attention. I can then identify when something is pulling at my heart strings or providing some sort of insight and direction. It's as if the subtle emotional or physical sensations are inviting me inward to access the truth and beauty within me.

I know the answers or solutions I'm looking for are not going to be found in a magic pill, and they don't set on the shelf of a superstore. My soul holds all the truth or answers I am looking for, and all I must do is inquire within and then honor the gift I am given.

We all love to be inspired, right? Who doesn't? Do you equally appreciate irritation and sadness? Or, do you do everything in your power to avoid feeling any sort of discomfort? Do you judge particular feelings as "wrong" and look for a fix or solution? If so, you could be passing up some of life's most valuable gifts, arising from the divine within you.

What if there was absolutely nothing to fix? What if you had no fear? What if there is no such thing as right or wrong, good or bad, or even truth, for that matter? What if what we think of as right, wrong, good, and bad are just assessments formed by the mind and have nothing to do with your ability to be happy? Then what? What would you choose to create of your own volition if you were capable of loving and embracing life exactly as it is—all of it?

What Sally, you, and I all have in common is our humanity. While we all have our own unique blend of delightful idiosyncrasies, all human beings collectively share the quality or condition of being human.

As we've already discussed in some depth, your thoughts and old subconscious programming control you unless you practice mindfulness and choose to direct your attention. Notice that I say "practice." It takes practice, and even though we know what we know, we sometimes forget or allow ourselves to get triggered by one thing or another, falling at the mercy of an automated reaction.

Past hurts, emotional triggers, and judgment all have a way of keeping us stuck. What they all share in common is that they are a product of a belief that something is wrong, that an experience or circumstance should be or should have been other than it is or was. It is the mind, the meaning-making machine, that labels an emotion as bad.

However, we often fail to realize we have assigned meaning. Instead, we get sucked into emotional turbulence that feels so real. Worse, we so easily interpret the way we feel as validation for the story we are telling ourselves. We think the hurt we feel is a result of something being done *to* us. Being free of all judgment and avoiding what I call "make wrong" is easier said than done. In complete honesty, who doesn't have a laundry list of complaints?

I once had a conversation with a man who had a certain way about him that I can't quite describe other than to say he looked unusually peaceful and content. I felt compelled to learn more about him. He shared with me that he recently completed a course that cost thirty-thousand dollars. Needless to say, I was intrigued and eager to discover what he learned . . . as if I could get thirty-thousand dollars in knowledge in one conversation with him. When I asked what he studied in the course, his answer was brief. He told me, with the biggest smile I've ever seen, that he learned to not "make wrong." It is a moment I will never forget. Ever since then, I've had heightened awareness of all the "make wrong" in the world. We judge everything.

Just think about this for a moment. If you're right about something, what's on the flip side? Wrong. If something is good, there must be something bad, right? Humans will do pretty much anything to be right or good—carefully avoiding the flip side: wrong and bad. Letting go of judgment and expectations, not labeling good and bad, allows us to move forward and creates space for true discernment and happiness.

How? Observe. When you notice emotional or physical stress (for example, feeling tied up in knots), there's a disempowering story you are telling yourself and buying into. Guaranteed, if you are upset, there is a belief that something is wrong, an expectation that life or a specific circumstance shouldn't be the way it is. This always creates unhappiness.

The power in observing is that you are able to discern when you are being impacted by the mind's rationalization. The human experience isn't happy all the time. Generating your own happiness is being able to observe and let go of whatever the ego is attached to. Happiness is being able to observe so you are no longer trapped by the story you're telling yourself or the meaning your mind is making. From the place of observer, it's possible to be in wonder and awe of what it is to be human. This is a great place to be.

When you have anxiety about a specific situation, it indicates you're attached to a desired outcome. Again, it's not bad. Your anxiety is a signal that you have a limiting or disempowering belief. When you observe the human, conditioned response, you can choose to appreciate or even find humor in the workings of the human mind. More importantly, you can recognize the emotion for what it is and then let it go.

Shifting from attachment to a specific outcome to discernment about your mind and emotions can be an art. You can close your eyes and take a deep breath, which allows your brain to idle for a moment by reducing the sensory stimulation. Then you can use self-questioning and curiosity to observe your reaction and determine what is motivating that reaction.

You can tell you are attached to an outcome when you feel anxiety, anger, fear, or frustration or when your feelings are hurt by another. These are all emotional responses to having a certain expectation. It will seem there is a right way and a wrong way for things to go; you'll have a clear verdict on the situation. You'll also notice you're spending a lot of time and energy processing or evaluating the factors influencing the situation. You are attached when you try to control, manipulate, or force certain outcomes. When you don't trust that whatever will be, will be, you are attached.

Attachment and judgment creates "stuckness." Discernment creates insight and possibility. Happiness lies in being in awe, wonder, and appreciation of all that is, as it is, and all that is possible to create.

I've been suggesting that you strengthen your ability to recognize the automatic, constant thinking mechanism within you (which is often negatively biased) so you can consciously choose where to direct your focus. This skill takes work. You can't simply turn off the voice that identifies itself as "I" and "me" (the ego), no matter how hard you try.

So, instead, I suggest you start by simply taking notice of the voice. Then, start to question, rather than believe everything the voice says. Ask yourself what you are saying to yourself and notice the corresponding state you're in, both your emotional state and how you feel physically. How are you responding to what you're telling yourself? Does it feel true to you?

By accepting we are prewired to work the way we do, versus wrestling to change that over which we have no control, our struggle and unhappiness dissolve. Only then are we able to create from nothing, versus trying to change something we judge as wrong or bad. I can assure you that if you go about trying to fix something you believe to be bad or wrong, you'll set yourself up to be disappointed with the outcome. Or, at a minimum, you'll be far less effective than if you come from a place of love. That's just the way life works.

For example, Sally has been dissatisfied with her job and her boss. She feels like she doesn't get credit for all her hard work, ideas, and contributions. She never gets the good assignments that keep her interested and engaged. Even though she daydreams about walking out and telling her boss how she honestly feels, she continues to go to work every day and bites her lip.

While we do have the ability to change many of our circumstances in life, many situations do not allow us to simply walk out or quit. For example, Sally's mom's Alzheimer's will continue to get progressively worse. There is no magic wand that can prevent this.

Sally does have a choice, however. She can resist and struggle with the circumstance in futility, or she can recognize it's perfectly normal to get frustrated, discouraged, and anxious sometimes. Accepting and acknowledging what she's dealing with is what creates peace of mind and space for action and new possibilities.

When Sally becomes defensive and makes a case against everything and everyone, she could reach out to someone and say, "Hey, I'm making myself absolutely nuts here. Can you please give me a few minutes of your time and attention to help me break this craziness I find myself in?" This works for me when I ask my husband for help—instead of putting friends, family, and coworkers on the witness stand to prosecute.

While it is theoretically possible for Sally to quit her job, it doesn't seem like a viable option. And, if she were to quit and find another job out of frustration, chances are, she would bring with her the same negativity that colors her experience at her current job. The more Sally tries to fix her situation by avoiding her boss, the more glaring all of her frustrations are. Looking for other openings and daydreaming about retirement only leaves her with more and more unfinished work at the end of each day. Sally thinks she is trying to fix her situation, but, despite her efforts, she finds herself in the same predicament day after day.

We aren't always in complete control of our thoughts, circumstances, or physical environment. Knowing this, why do we tend to take things so personally? Why do we tend to struggle and resist that over which we have little to no control? The *why* doesn't matter, actually. The value is in noticing *what* we do when we react and resist.

Start by accepting yourself and honoring the challenges that come with being human. They are here to teach you and take you to the next level. You are in charge of your own peace and happiness. "Overwhelm" is just a word and has no real power over you. You are always able to rise above the chaos to a place of gratitude. As you know, your blessings far outweigh your challenges.

Notice when you make an argument about something because you want to be right. Think about what you're creating for the person on the flip side. Is pushing someone to defend herself against being wrong your intention? Probably not, but don't be surprised when you're faced with hostility.

When you catch yourself in this struggle, you can give up the fight to be right. Let it go, and you will experience a peaceful calm. It's amazing. When we stop encouraging our mind's natural defensiveness, something interesting and wonderful happens—we enter the present moment.

Have you ever noticed, when you're in a disagreement with someone or have experienced a conflict of some sort, that you spend a lot of time explaining and defending your version of the story? The ego has a dire need to be right. It wants to justify our feelings and interpretation of the situation. But, no matter how hard we try, we aren't ever in complete control. We can't command others to like us, and we can't ensure we are always right. We're not in charge of others or the environment. We're not empowered to alter all aspects of our world. By accepting this, we can alleviate some of our struggle. We can stop taking life so personally.

I choose to believe that we are here on earth as humans for the full experience and adventure of being human. I believe our biggest limitations do not come from circumstances but rather from limiting beliefs about who we are and what we are capable of doing. I also believe the ego doesn't like the unknown, yet, ironically, the willingness to enter into the unknown is quite possibly the fastpass to generating your own happiness.

LET'S PLAY:

- WHAT/WHO HAVE YOU BEEN MAKING WRONG? ARE YOU WILLING TO LET GO OF ASSESSING AND PROSECUTING?

- TO WHAT OUTCOME ARE YOU CURRENTLY ATTACHED?

- WITHOUT FEELING LIKE THERE WAS SOMETHING WRONG THAT NEEDED TO BE FIXED, WHAT COULD YOU CREATE?

CHAPTER 19

⌒

MEET YOUR SOUL

WE'VE DISCUSSED THAT SALLY feels disconnected from herself and the life she actually wants. What does this mean? What exactly is she disconnected *from*?

Sally has been living life in a mechanical manner, doing the same dutiful routine. She has been prioritizing what is "right" without checking in with her own personal truth or what she wants. Not only has she neglected checking in with what's important to her, she hasn't trusted that the true answers are within her. She has trusted her ability to perform and follow the rules—rather than honoring her inner intelligence. She has learned to ignore herself and instead follow societal expectations.

While following the rules has kept her out of trouble, she has missed out on pursuing her passions, purpose, and fulfillment. Because she was never taught how to access her own truth, Sally hasn't acknowledged or explored her God-given ability to have a direct connection with infinite wisdom. She doesn't know she can create what she wants in her life.

Do any of these statements resonate with your current experience? You may have chosen this book because you are dissatisfied in your day-to-day routine. You may know, deep down, there is something deep within you that needs to be addressed. While reading, have you identified an inner ache? Have you identified thoughts and beliefs that may be blocking your success? If so, there is no better time than the present to face these feelings head on. If not, open yourself up to the possibility there is more for you in life.

Like Sally, the vast majority of us suffer the consequences of being disconnected from inner truth and infinite wisdom, though we may not realize it. We may think we know what is important to us, and many people will defend what they have been taught to believe at all costs. However, that's just the human desire to be right. We fear criticism. This is why people will defend a position that may not be in their best interest or even beneficial to the greater good.

It takes effort to question what we've been taught, our traditions or habits. Many of the beliefs we defend have been passed down generation after generation, from those we love and trust most. It takes intention, hard work, and tenacity to examine these beliefs and find what is true for you, but before you give up, please know this is a crucial step in generating your own genuine happiness.

So how do you do this? How do you determine the values and passions that truly resonate with your soul? What is a "soul" anyway? Up until now, I've referenced your "inner compass", but you may call it spirit, inner being, universal wisdom, or God connection. I personally think of soul guidance as a form of intuition, which is why I've used the term "inner compass." However, I will use the word "soul" for the discussion in this chapter. You can call it what you want. After all, we are doing our best to explain the unexplainable.

Your soul is the non-physical, eternal, all-powerful part of you that allows you to connect to the divine spirit. It connects your consciousness to your intuition. The soul communicates or guides you with a subtle knowing, giving you a yes or no, a subtle nudge that draws your attention to something, making you feel a yearning.

I invite you to consider that your soul is who you actually are—not just a part of your inner life. It is the keeper and creator of real happiness. It is the greatest expression of love through you, although often the most forgotten or unexpressed part of ourselves. This is the missing link. We miss out on happiness because we are disconnected from our soul. It's time to meet your soul.

I offer you an invitation to grow spiritually and mentally. You can learn to express your inner being in a way that allows your greater soul happiness to arise. To do this, let's discuss the differences between mind, heart, and soul and consider where we commonly get confused.

The issue, for most, is we don't realize or we forget that we are soul, that we carry a conscious life force within our bodies. We don't trust that we *are* this faculty and have a spiritual presence within us. We can express who we are as soul through our human experience.

Many people confuse having an ah-ha moment with accessing the soul because of the expansive feeling they have when they get a new realization or discover a solution. But really, an ah-ha moment is a sudden realization or insight where the mind replaces one belief with a new belief it likes more. There is no soul connection when you replace one belief with another. It's simply a thought process; we are exchanging an old thought for a new one. It's still the mind thinking.

The mind is not the soul, and having an ah-ha thought is uniquely different from accessing your soul. True, insight is the brain's ability to solve a problem that typically cannot be solved with conventional or logical reasoning, but it still originates in the mind. On the other hand, the soul expresses itself inside the unknown. It finds happiness and freedom within creativity or creation in all its forms.

Through creativity, we express happiness, and true happiness comes from our true being. Creativity is the process of leaving prescribed thinking to pursue the unknown. It requires exploration and openness and, in turn, allows our happiness to be expressed fully. Through honing our skills to create and to imagine *what if*, we step into our inner greatness and release happiness.

When we make a daring plan, or pick up the paint brush, tool, or instrument to create, we allow the expression of our soul to come alive. When this happens, our mind does what it was supposed to do in the first place—that is, it assists the soul in creation, rather than controlling or dominating the whole show. People often call this experience "being in the zone" or "in flow." It's a state of being that has focus and joy. It is quiet and effortless. Creation is simply expression.

The feeling of *knowing* that produces the thought, *Yes, true,* is your soul. This silent intelligence is what people call the muse. It just comes seemingly out of nowhere. This is your soul. The thing about your soul is that it's quiet and still. It's not emotional, and it's not mind chatter. It's not the voice in your head. The soul has quiet knowing.

We aren't often able to access that quiet knowing because our mind, filled with defensiveness and blame, is usually running the show. The issue for most is that they are looking outside themselves for guidance and answers. We are trained to look for the exterior solution, the three steps to _____ (you name it). We think that following someone else's proven formula will lead us to happiness. Though hard to accept, there are no right answers outside yourself, no one-size-fits-all solution to magically dissolve or prevent life's woes.

While some mistake the mind for the soul, others confuse their soul with their emotional center—but there is a vast difference. While being mindful of what pulls at your heartstrings is telling, feelings are not your soul. Rather, emotions are great indicators that you have a belief and are making meaning out of that belief.

I prefer to use "heart" to refer to emotion, even though feelings are technically generated by your limbic system, and our brainstem controls the impulses sent to our body. The second you give a thing or experience meaning, emotions well up, and you experience emotional and physiological feelings. If you don't assign meaning, emotions don't come up. So, if "your heart isn't in it", you will feel no emotional connection to a task or idea.

The heart allows us to experience a connection between the physical sensations of our body and the emotions that arise in response to our assessments of the world. Our emotional responses can be telling. Likewise, they can be deceiving. That's why I encourage you to ask what you're telling yourself when you experience negative emotions. Emotions are linked to beliefs and can reveal when a belief you hold is disempowering you or, conversely, when something is meaningful to you.

Emotional responses can be triggered for what seems like no apparent reason. For example, someone can be offended when someone says or does something against what he considers to be right or appropriate. To the person being triggered, his emotional reaction seems perfectly justified. He doesn't see the personal, instantaneous association he made that set him off.

Mindfulness allows you to recognize your emotional and physiological responses as indicators that you have a belief or judgment that is either empowering or disempowering you. Joy is a specific indicator, letting you know where to go next in life. Pay attention to whatever makes you feel joyful, passionate, excited, and fully alive. Your heart usually knows more than your rational mind.

Many people say they are following their heart, when really they are following their soul. Soul resonance is what feels good; it's the gut check that gives the heart a feeling of alignment. Suddenly, you get a yes or a no—you just know. If you follow soul's guidance, you feel good. If you don't follow it, you get mind chatter that leads to rationalization, criticism, and blame. It happens in a nanosecond.

For example, when we are inspired, we experience a desire to do something, or we have an idea about what we want to create. This desire is accompanied by an enlivened physical state, a feeling. Being inspired means your soul is aligned with your spirit; you may feel guided by divine influence. Inspiration is followed by motivation, excitement, and other positive emotions. This is how we can so easily confuse positive emotion with soul because you experience positive emotion when you honor your soul.

Your soul is who you are; it's your eternal being or spirit, your essence. Your soul doesn't have neurotic, unhealthy thinking—but your mind does. Remember, the voice of your ego is not the voice of your soul. It can be challenging to tell the difference between the two, and confusion can result in unhappiness.

The voice of your ego is concerned with physical and emotional survival. For example, your ego wants you to have a secure job and savings for retirement, while the voice of your soul may yearn to be expressed through art or by sharing your unique gifts with the world. Your ego is the part of you that wants to be in a place of safety and familiarity. It wants to make smart, sensible plans and urges you to be watchful against things that may be risky or emotionally hurtful. Your ego cares what other people think.

You can tell your ego is running the show when you feel worried, nervous, or inadequate. It can also generate the opposite feelings: dominance, superiority, and self-righteousness. Soul doesn't do this. Soul happiness is a knowingness, a sense of alignment and warmth in your heart.

As we've discussed, choosing what you tell yourself is powerful. Yet, it's not related to what we're discussing when I refer to the soul. It's easy to confuse the power of your soul with the power of being able to direct how you think and feel. We are often taught positive thinking techniques, yet we are not taught how to access and honor our soul. We're not usually taught how to direct our focus and attention to support the soul or how to create intention in our thinking and speaking that will resonate with the soul.

Many people hear their thoughts and think it's a message from God or from their soul. While some may receive guidance or an intuitive knowing, the soul isn't a voice in your head. The soul doesn't contemplate or evaluate. The messages we receive as if from a divine voice, which seem so profound, can be confusing. Though insight is wonderful, it is still part of the function of the mind. Insights are a testimony to the complexity of the brain, which is a marvel—but it is not the soul.

The human mind is a set of cognitive faculties, including perception, thinking, judgment, and memory. While extremely valuable and essential for our survival, the intellect also creates self-deception and false beliefs. The human mind likes control and wants to create familiarity and safety; the soul does not. The soul observes and listens and is the part of you that is okay with the unknown. True happiness is created from your soul because it is in true alignment with the divine.

The mind is the element that enables a person to think and be aware of the world and their experiences. It is a person's intellect. The processing of the mind can't know or recognize the soul (the divine part of our human experience); it can only conceptualize the soul as the spiritual or immaterial part of our being. The mind also rules the ego, a person's sense of self-importance and identity. The ego is the part of you that speaks in "I", that creates the illusion that we are separate from the divine.

If your soul is you, your true essence, and knows your likes and dislikes and is the thing that makes happiness possible, then how do you access your soul? The key is to be aware of your inner life. Practice mindfulness so you can recognize the function of your mind and your emotions and keep those processes distinct from your soul happiness. Go to www.generatingyourownhappiness.com for my personal mindfulness techniques and feel free to add any of my practices to your own.

You know your ego mind is in charge when the following things occur:

- Your sense of worth is based on external factors, like how much money you have, your image, or living up to certain social expectations.
- You experience emotional reactions (e.g., your feelings are hurt; you're angry or upset when things don't go your way; you're nervous).
- You find yourself overanalyzing something.
- You care what others think and seek validation from others.

We all have an ego, but you don't have to believe what it says. When you catch your ego, your personal attorney making its case for something, try not to take it too seriously. It's not the real you; it's just part of being human. You may even laugh.

When your soul is in charge and your mind is assisting your soul, you may experience the following:

- You love and accept yourself deeply and completely.
- You feel connected to and appreciate the world around you.
- You have love and compassion for people and things as they are.
- You get a gut feeling about things, an intuition, an inner voice

which guides you.

- You have a sense of yearning or a burning desire to create, without attachment to or association with self-worth.
- You get a feeling of being in flow or of being one with.
- Life's events seem to have synchronicity (you notice and enjoy seemingly magical coincidences).

LET'S PLAY:

- DO YOU EXPERIENCE FLOW AS YOU GO ABOUT YOUR JOB OR PERSONAL ROUTINE?

- CAN YOU IDENTIFY AN AREA OF YOUR LIFE IN WHICH THE EGO IS IN CHARGE?

- CAN YOU IDENTIFY AN EXPERIENCE YOU'VE HAD THAT ORIGINATED WITH YOUR SOUL?

CHAPTER 20

QUESTIONS AND
CONTEMPLATION

THOUGHTFUL QUESTIONS AND CONTEMPLATION are powerful tools to help you access your own truth and soul guidance. This kind of contemplation grants you access to what matters most, to what lights you up and feeds your soul.

Questioning is the conscious act of asking a question in order to discover information. Contemplation is sitting with a question and exploring or observing it from an unbiased perspective, without making it right or wrong. Contemplation is a form of introspection in which the whole sensory system allows for reflecting, which is very different from evaluating or assessing. Contemplation is being with a question without pushing it, allowing your mind to start making connections, start creating images and ideas, and possibly even provide an answer for a question you have had for a while.

This is how you have those ah-ha moments of insight. Between thoughts, you may experience a subtle sense of knowing, direction, or soul guidance. The "yes" or "no" response you receive in your gut or heart during the process of contemplation comes from your soul.

Inquiry and contemplation are distinctly different from meditation, which is also a great practice to facilitate insight and mindfulness. Meditation is a practice of directing your focus, most commonly on your breath, to create the absence of thinking about the external world and events taking place around you. It is a discipline of quieting the mind and creating mindfulness. When thoughts come up, you dismiss them. Meditation is a great practice to build awareness and stillness of the mind so you can identify your soul more clearly.

Here's an example of inquiry and contemplation. You may inquire by asking yourself a question like, *How do I help my body heal?* The brain begins searching for an answer. And that's what we want. We're not thinking about the errand we need to run on the way home from work; we are not hung up on the reason we don't have what we want or how someone has let us down. Rather, focused attention on the question, *How do I help my body heal?*, sends your mind on an errand to solve this puzzle. The mind can feel your intention, and you can feel your mind as it races for an answer.

Inquiry and contemplation isn't defensive and it does not have a biased motive. For example, you may be questioning what you want out of life. You could ask yourself, *What do I want next?* There's no fear in asking, and there is no right or wrong answer. Contemplation is being with the question long enough for the creative force within you to supply answers. Sometimes it gives you one answer, but most often it gives you multiple answers. You are talking with and allowing the soul to come forth.

Contemplation unleashes creativity and imagination that's not muddied by making meaning or by assessment and fear. On the other hand, meditation stills the incessant thinking and chatter of the mind and allows your soul to simply observe and witness what is happening. You notice without judgment.

Meditation, contemplation, and inquiry are all important, yet distinct, practices. Here's another example to help you distinguish the differences. Suppose you have a thought, *I'm feeling anxious.* Inquiry would ask, *Why am I feeling anxious? What am I telling myself?* In contemplation, you sit with those questions and wait for answers. When you get the right answer, you feel it in your soul, not in your mind. Your mind will keep giving you thoughts until you say, *Yes, that's it.* In meditation, however, you have the thought, *I'm feeling anxious,* and respond, *That's just a thought; come back to breathing.*

Inquiry is the act of asking for information, the ability to ask deep questions. Contemplation is the ability to sit with the questions and allow answers to surface. Meditation tames your thinking so you can observe and witness. Learning to quite the mind through meditation and practicing inquiry and contemplation allows you to identify what lights you up and feeds your soul. These three practices are powerful, so let's explore them more extensively.

Building self-awareness and learning mindfulness disciplines to quiet the mind, like meditation, are especially valuable. Meditation can help you notice your thoughts as an observer. Notice how life occurs for you and your corresponding thoughts, beliefs, and associations. Question everything. Don't automatically accept others' opinions and advice. Check in with yourself to see what rings true for you.

When we are unwilling to adopt a more curious, less judgmental point of view, we will soon be unhappy. Unhappiness is our power struggle with what is. Happiness is the natural state of your soul because the soul does not argue with the here and now. Only the mind assigns meaning to and argues with what is.

Ask, *What am I telling myself?* Notice how the message is making you feel. Notice what thoughts pull at your heartstrings. Notice the thoughts that can move you to tears. Notice what you find compelling. Notice what brings you a sense of true joy and passion. Then go deeper. Ask a question and then be silent. Allow the guidance you're seeking to come through. Remember, the soul doesn't speak to you in full-blown sentences, with reasoning and justification, nor does it ramble on. That being said, you can use your conscious mind to focus your attention. Answers come through when you ask and then listen.

The soul doesn't only speak to you in solitude. It can speak whenever you're open, receptive, and in the present moment. You can get answers when sitting in silence, while enjoying a hike, or while listening intently to people in conversation. The more you notice and take action in support of the guidance you receive, the more you will experience these intuitive experiences. Cherish these moments and enjoy true soul happiness.

In my personal experience (without the aid of psychedelic substances!), my soul speaks to me with an intuitive knowing. I have also experienced a tingling sensation in my arms and thighs, like goosebumps. I interpret the sensations as a sort of confirmation or subtle nudge to pay close attention to something in that moment. I also sometimes experience a subtle contrast in my listening, in which something briefly stands out, such as a person's name or a short phrase. If I hear any particular word in my mind, it's a "yes" response, like an acknowledgement. What I'm describing isn't always consistent. I've had experiences of heightened sensitivity and other times I hardly notice.

I like to keep a notebook with me to write down and capture my thoughts. As I write stream-of-consciousness style, bits and pieces will stand out to me in some subtle way, so I take notice. If I receive any words, it may be a simple "yes" or "that's it." If I can offer any guidance to those who are confused or not relating to what I describe, I would say listen *between* your thoughts, not *to* your thoughts.

The happiness piece, for me, is in honoring that which speaks to me and cherishing my experiences, both grand and small, as special gifts. I honor the gift of intuition by acknowledging it and acting on it. The more I do this, it seems the more I'm given.

I've been known to locate a stranger and invite her to lunch, sharing honestly that I simply had a sense I should meet her. I have acknowledged the tingling sensations in the midst of someone sharing something personal with me—just in case there was something for him to notice, too. And, as I shared earlier, I have taken on projects, like writing this book, to honor a sense of knowing that it was my next step (after having practiced inquiry and contemplation in an area that touched my heart). Through my experiences, I have come to believe the happiness we are pursuing is an ability to access our own truth within.

You may be wondering, *How do I discern when the sensation or thought is true or when it's a cunning deception?* Pay attention to your physical and emotional sensations; listen to your heart. I believe truth shows up as love or as an expression of love, beauty, and goodness. Anything other than love—negativity, justification, blame, make-wrong, fixation on what you don't want—is not true guidance from your soul. Rather, it's part of a seductive illusion.

Perhaps the greatest causes of unhappiness are the lies we tell ourselves and our penchant to "make wrong." Other contributors are the things we are taught or learn that are inconsistent with our soul's true desires. To modern society, happiness is a life that is safe, familiar, and easy, one without challenges. When we enter realms of unfamiliar territory, most people get anxious and interpret their physical and emotional symptoms as indicators that something is wrong. The ego, whose role is to defend and protect, makes a convincing argument to fight or flee. Most often, the ego tries to keep everything as is. The intentions of the ego are good, but the outcome is not.

Read this next thought carefully as it is my central message here: I believe, ultimately, our pursuit of happiness is a longing for and desire to receive love, express love, and be an expression of love. Let that sink in. See if it resonates with your soul—just as we've been discussing.

Anything other than love is the ego, our thinking part that gives us a sense of personal identity. It is the reasoning mind that I previously referred to as our personal attorney. Thoughts and beliefs about who we think we are can be far from the truth; they are merely ideas, conceptualized versions of who and what we imagine ourselves to be.

Most people believe their mind and the image of themselves generated there. They trust the ego, which justifies their persona and blames others for any shortcomings. Again, this tendency is not wrong or bad, it's just part of being human. It's part of our self-identity or self-defense. It's part of our built-in survival mechanism. If you direct your focus and bring curiosity and inquiry to this instinctual response, you may be fascinated by your own humanity. I am.

Consider that nothing of the mind is true. Beliefs are nothing but ideas and opinions, and they are fleeting, changing all the time. Consider that the "problem" or the challenge in the game we call life is that we take these beliefs to be true. Always be ready to ask yourself, *What rings true for me?* I appreciate John O'Donohue's thoughts on soul awareness from his book *Anam Cara: A Book of Celtic Wisdom:*

> *"Once the soul awakens, the search begins and you can never go back. From then on, you are inflamed with a special longing that will never again let you linger in the lowlands of complacency and partial fulfillment. The eternal makes you urgent. You are loath to let compromise or the threat of danger hold you back from striving toward the summit of fulfillment."*

LET'S PLAY:

- WHAT QUESTIONS DO YOU HAVE? PRACTICE INQUIRY AND CONTEMPLATION. DON'T FORGET TO TAKE ACTION AND HONOR THE GIFTS YOU'RE GIVEN. YOUR JOB IS TO HONOR AND FEED YOUR SOUL.

- ASK YOURSELF, *HOW CAN I RECEIVE LOVE, EXPRESS LOVE, AND BE AN EXPRESSION OF LOVE RIGHT NOW, WITHOUT CHANGING ANYTHING?*

CHAPTER 21

JUST DO IT

WE'VE REACHED THE PLACE where I must remind you that action is key. True growth, expansion of perspective, and genuine happiness come through experience, and experience requires you to act. There is no other way.

It is no wonder Nike's slogan, "Just Do It", has been so successful and stood the test of time. It's authentic and powerful. It resonates with positive feelings, values, and desires and inspires action. Deep down, we know there is no other way to accomplish anything other than to just do it. Yet, we get tangled up in life's complexities, and it becomes less clear. You likely wish life *could* be as simple as the slogan. The truth is, when we're inspired, it's as if we have no limits and can perform miracles, but when we're discouraged, doing even the smallest task can seem daunting.

Life is not intended to be simple. Life will never be all sunshine and rainbows, a positive arc of just-do-it buoyancy. After all, the objective is not to avoid or prevent all pain. There is no reward in a life that's always easy. Instead, happiness comes alive through honoring what speaks to your soul and overcoming the obstacles along the way. One of our greatest sources of authentic power comes from our willingness to act in the face of obstacles.

When you step into generating something bigger than you previously considered, ugly, painful emotions and old, limiting beliefs often surface. It can feel like an attack. However, resistance to this process only causes more pain. Instead, allow and embrace whatever comes up. Openness will create a sense of peace and contentment that allows old hurts to be released.

When you honor what your divine soul wants by following your inner compass, you will likely enter new, unfamiliar territory. It takes courageous action to step outside of the box. It can be scary, and your ego may become uncomfortable, especially as you get closer to achieving a big goal. When you challenge your ego, your sense of identity and your previous assumptions are threatened.

When stepping out of your comfort zone or bringing to fruition that which spoke to you on a deep level, it's amazing how distractions rush in to pull you away. For example, you may decide to clean out a drawer or organize a closet—something completely off task—but suddenly urgent. Or, your sexy excuses may entice you, throwing up roadblocks and making you reconsider. Sometimes organizing your desk can help you regain a sense of order and control, but more often than not, you'll only find another distraction that leads you further from your goal. Worse, you may fall into a disempowering mindset, in which you second-guess yourself and feel discouraged.

I call these traps "stuck points." Stuck points can be painful and debilitating. So, how do you break through a stuck point? The answer seems clear: you *just do it*. We know that when we choose to push through perceived limits and step out onto the skinny branches, we always grow and learn, regardless of the outcome. Yet, it seems we forget the potential benefits and thus become discouraged. Doing it, moving forward, all at once seems impossible.

In times like these, the renovation exercises you learned in chapter twelve can help you to shift your mindset. You must be able to regain control of your mind so it supports your inner compass and higher goal, rather than allowing your rational mind to run the show.

Hopefully, you've had many great insights as you've related to Sally's life. You may even be wondering if she managed to get out of debt since her coming-clean moment with her sister. Let's look at Sally's life one more time.

Since Sally opened up to her sister, her sister has become more involved in their mom's care. They sat down together and came up with a plan. Her sister has also increased her visits, easing the burden for Sally and alleviating much of Sally's stress.

Initiating change by facing her debt and speaking directly with her sister was a major turning point for Sally. Those actions inspired more action. She successfully cut back expenses, implemented a monthly budget to pay off her debt, and found a replacement for her volunteer position at the children's hospital. Before leaving the hospital, she headed up training sessions for the onboarding of new leadership. She was also inspired to do deep cleaning at home, and donated some great treasures to a local nonprofit to benefit foster children.

While purging these items, she felt a compelling desire to clean up other areas of her life. She decided she had outgrown her career and yearned for something more fulfilling. She felt called to start her own business, one that would make a difference in the world. She was excited and had a newfound energy. She stayed up late, searching the web for ideas and resources. Then she would spring awake at four in the morning with more ideas and an urge to keep working. Day after day, she fell asleep with her computer next to her, and she filled the notebook she carried in her purse.

She was drawn to the inspiration found in nature. She wanted to eat healthier and take better care of her body, too. For the first time, she wasn't eating to lose or maintain her weight. She was eating for optimum health, and she loved it. She started walking twice a week with an old friend and was reminded of how much their friendship meant to her.

It was as if everything was falling into place. She experienced synchronicity and was in awe of the many meaningful, related events which occurred. The connections and flow were more than coincidence. For example, she was introduced to a life coach just when she sensed it was time to build her support network.

Sally was on a high for the first time in a long time. She was experiencing an exciting time of transformation and was evolving into someone she had not previously known herself to be. She could hardly believe she was once Sally Stuck-in-a-Rut. She was releasing old beliefs and limiting ways of living; she felt free from her past. She felt deeply connected to people and nature and experienced a feeling of oneness.

People noticed the change in Sally. Some wanted to know what she was doing. Whatever it was, they wanted it too. However, some family members were not at all supportive. They were dubious and tried to caution her. In their estimation, her vision was an unattainable pipe dream, and she was being self-centered. They told her to get her priorities straight and warned she would be a fool to jeopardize her career.

At first, she shrugged off the negativity, but it ate away at her. Her family was important to her, and she couldn't understand why they weren't supportive. The relationships that should've provided comfort were now strained.

This pattern is all too common. When you begin to change, tension often arises in those relationships closest to you. It's hard to remember we are each on our own soul journey, taking on different roles and expanding at different rates. Just because you are ready, it doesn't mean your loved ones will be, too. If you expect them to change with you or even to applaud you, you are likely setting yourself up for disappointment. To quote the Dalai Lama, "People take different roads seeking fulfillment and happiness. Just because they're not on your road does not mean they are lost."

Several weeks passed, and Sally hadn't touched her business plan, though it was close to completion. Everything else took priority. Work was demanding, and no one was capable of assuming her role after she left. If she left now, her entire department would suffer. Her son was having problems at school and needed more attention. She had stopped attending the events for the children's hospital, had not maintained her friendships with the other volunteers, and was feeling incredibly lonely. To make matters worse, she began having severe abdominal cramps, nausea, and general fatigue.

Neither her doctor nor the gastrointestinal specialist had been able to find anything wrong or make a diagnosis.

She started second-guessing everything—especially her ability to pull off being self-employed. Though ninety percent of the hard work of making a business plan was done, her vision suddenly seemed hopeless. Even almost being debt free wasn't exciting to her. Her motivation and confidence had disappeared.

Have you had a similar experience? When pressures start to mount, the overwhelming majority of people quit, giving up on what had previously inspired them. So many stray from their path out of fear, which is cleverly disguised as practicality. Their dream seems impossibly out of reach and ridiculous to expect, so they dare not go for it.

Let's look at what Sally experiences as she hits her stuck point:

- She's physically and mentally exhausted.
- She's easily irritated.
- She's judgmental of everything and everyone.
- She feels alone.
- She's procrastinating and pretending like everything else is more important.
- She thinks her original goal is too hard.

Overall, no matter how hard she pushes herself, she can't go forward. It seems like a dark cloud is hanging over her. She knows she's capable of more, but somehow she lets discouragement take her down.

So how does Sally get out of this funk? Should she quit, or can she overcome the hurdles? This is where having a coach is golden for Sally. She may not know how to prevent getting stuck, but with the right support, she can get unstuck.

Starting her own business doesn't have a deadline like her corporate day job often has. Her company sets deadlines with clients, and if the deliverables aren't met on time, there is a monetary penalty to the company. If Sally doesn't deliver at work, her department's jobs are on the line. This is one reason Sally's personal goals have been put on the back burner.

How do you establish accountability for yourself if you don't have an external consequence, like a tax deadline, court date, or a customer breathing down your neck? How do you push through your stuck point when there isn't a "have to" being imposed by an outside force?

Most would say that you need to have skin in the game, something at stake. For example, paying for coaching is a good way to solidify your commitment to change. You then have a financial investment, and there is someone expecting you to deliver. Just knowing someone is watching can kick the ego into action since people generally don't want to look bad. But, that's not always enough. Once you break one promise, breaking future promises is far more likely. Statistically, people fail at hitting their goals more often than not, and often end up hiding from the person they asked to hold them to account.

Sally's issue isn't accountability as she has accountability with her coach. Rather, Sally is avoiding something. She's listening to the voice in her head that's saying, *It's hard. Let's get out of the game.*

She's close to accomplishing her goal of launching a business that reso-nates with her soul, but she can't quite see it. Or can she? Maybe she's frightened by the unknown that lies ahead. Often, we can't see for ourselves that what we're working for is just on the other side of one more small hill. Instead, we let our imagination and fear stop us. We think we don't have what is needed to make it.

Stuck points are created by what you are saying to yourself. Perhaps Sally was saying these phrases to herself:

- "This sucks."
- "It's hard."
- "I don't know what to do."

Somehow, we think life shouldn't be hard or scary. When you get close to a major breakthrough that requires stepping outside of your comfort zone, your mind can coerce you into playing it safe. Your mind and ego help you survive, and the unknown is perceived as a threat. If you leave the choice to change to your clever ego, you'll be led into self-sabotage. This happens to many people.

To fight back, use the turn-around exercise from chapter twelve to ask a few questions: What if your ego is the only thing standing between where you are now and the new reality you envisioned? What if the struggle is a trial or challenge to test your faith and commitment? How badly do you want a new reality? Are you willing to do whatever it takes, or are you going to quit?

Feelings of sadness and heightened emotion are normal when you are headed down an unfamiliar path or up to something big. Although the process can be difficult, it's helpful to allow the emotions to surface and to embrace the discomfort. This is not the time to resist and stuff your emotions. Resisting this part of your journey will allow your fears to hold you back. This is where most people quit and return to an unfulfilling life, accepting the status quo.

Take a deep breath and let go of any resistance. Trust in yourself and the divine to guide you. You don't need to know how. It's time to step out in faith and just do it.

We know how satisfying it is to have a big win after putting in hard work, sweat, and tears, but we forget. We try to teach our kids this lesson by telling stories of shoveling snow and working while going to school to buy our first beater car. But then we give them a conflicting message by providing them with things instead of having them go through the pain of sacrifice and hard work. We don't want life to be hard for them and think it should be easy for us now, too.

An Olympic athlete knows it's not supposed to be easy. The coach has done the hard work before, but the athlete has to go through it for himself. There is no other way. Watch any feel-good, sports-themed movie, and it will reinforce this truth: hard work precedes victory. Yet, we forget.

This inclination to forget is why a good coach is crucial—if you are willing to be coachable. We are often able to trust another when we second-guess ourselves. With support, we're able to test our own limits, knowing if we start to drown there is someone to pull us up.

Let me be clear, though. There is a big difference in being coachable while following your inner compass versus discounting your own knowing and following someone else's advice. A good coach won't actually tell you what to do. Instead, they will support you in the process of listening to yourself. They may ask questions or nudge and encourage you to take action, but they can't do the heavy lifting for you. Only you can generate your own happiness.

Overcoming or moving through your stuck point requires two things: surrendering to whatever it is you're dealing with and letting go of the idea that something is wrong if you struggle. You must display tenacity in the face of your discomfort. You must be willing to embrace the part of the journey that's hard and the part of you that's afraid. You must trust you're on the right path. Few things are more fulfilling than overcoming this stage.

Sally's problem is her own self-sabotage. Her sense of doubt is not a figment of her imagination. What she's dealing with is real. Yet there is a difference in Sally when she's empowered with a bring-it-on approach versus her "I just don't know how much more I can handle" mindset. The latter is an expression of Sally feeling powerless and being the victim. When in the midst of a stuck point, it may seem like life is happening *to* you instead of feeling you're at the helm of your life.

It's amazing how much we can actually handle. While writing this book, I experienced more "bad luck" within a three-month period than over the span of the previous decade. There was a lot to deal with, many fires to put out, but I was in awe of the series of events, not taken out by them. Then, with the drama behind me and life back to "normal", I found myself procrastinating in more than one area for no apparent reason.

Yep. I had slipped into my own stuck point. I was close to completing this book; my lighting company was ready to roll out new information to our customers; I had accountability in place . . . yet I was stalling. Sure enough, my coach confronted me, and I experienced all the emotions of the powerless little girl deep inside.

I learned to embrace this type of emotion and vulnerability, rather than stuff it. Sure, I've been uncomfortable. I've wished there was a way to prevent or overcome hurdles without feeling choked up or having snot running out of my nose, but that's just the way it is when I am about to break through to happiness. This is how struggle, then victory, shows up for me.

But that period of doubt and fear doesn't mean I'm weak. If anything, the emotional release has a beneficial purpose. I've learned to welcome any sadness or deep emotion and let it go, even though I can still get embarrassed and self-conscious at times. Fortunately, I know emotional freedom and empowerment is on the other side of feeling stuck. I've learned to trust there is light at the end of the tunnel.

What I find fascinating is that when you're in the midst of a stuck point, it can feel like you are in a haze. You feel bogged down, and the simplest of tasks feels incredibly daunting. When you step through it, however, it's like the fog lifts, and you are able to see clearly. Bad feelings and problems seem to magically disappear. It's such a great experience that songs are written about it. To generate happiness, sometimes all you need is willingness to let go.

I'll close this chapter with a quote from Achaan Chah: "If you let go a little, you will have a little happiness. If you let go a lot, you will have a lot of happiness. And if you let go completely, you will be free."

LET'S PLAY:

- WHAT DISTRACTIONS ARE CURRENTLY THREATENING TO PULL YOU AWAY FROM YOUR GOAL?

- WHAT CHANGE MUST YOU INITIATE TO GET PAST YOUR STUCK POINT AND JUST DO IT?

- DO YOU HAVE THE SUPPORT OF A COACH THAT'S THE RIGHT FIT FOR YOU TO HELP YOU PUSH PAST ANY HURDLES?

CHAPTER 22

SETTING UP YOUR SUPPORT STRUCTURE

YOU NOW KNOW THE pitfalls that lead to unhappiness, and you know generating your own happiness is an ongoing process. So, what's next?

I've said it a number of times: there is no one-size-fits-all approach to generating your own happiness. However, for each of us, a support structure is always necessary. Without a strong support structure, you'll likely revert to being stuck in a rut and "shoulding" yourself about it.

Let's use the analogy of laying a foundation when building a house. Without a solid foundation, the house won't have structural integrity. But with a sound foundation, with support from the ground up, it can withstand the wildest storm. I want you to lay a secure foundation that will anchor you as you chase your wildest dream. I want you to identify and recruit support.

You will need support as you reach beyond your comfort zone and honor your inner compass. You will encounter rocky terrain throughout your adventure, but your support will fortify you for the journey. By making happiness a priority, you will benefit from a life of purpose. You will be empowered to create anything your heart desires.

Rather than judging and making wrong, you can learn to identify behavioral, emotional, physical, and language cues that indicate you are creating a victim mentality and solidifying a limiting belief. By practicing letting go and being in a state of inquiry instead of justification mode, you can be present to these indicators and know they are opportunities to identify what is important to you.

When you notice these indicators and hear your own disempowering language, you can act, because you now know how to turn this energy around. With practice, you'll be able to trust in yourself and push through sexy excuses and self-sabotage. If in doubt, ask yourself what you're saying to yourself and what you want. Then listen. Pay attention and notice when you get a sense of *knowing*. It comes from your gut, your soul. When you connect with your inner compass, honor it by taking action.

We've learned so much together. I trust you're going to break through to more happiness and fulfillment than you've ever experienced before. However, no one should walk this path alone. You are empowered with knowledge, but you must continue to build support so you consistently move forward. There is much you can personally do to stay unstuck, but never underestimate the power of outside support.

If your life was optimized for happiness, success, and well-being, what would it look like? What structures and practices should you put in place to support that goal? Here is what currently works for me:

- Accepting one-on-one coaching
- Participating in a small group for accountability and comradery
- Dumping mental data (a stream-of-consciousness-style to-do-list)
- Being in a leadership role within a community
- Creating something with determination

- Scheduling social time with family and friends
- Practicing meditation
- Continuing education, including reading, audio books, podcasts, classes, and seminars
- Prioritizing physical activity (of which I particularly enjoy attending group fitness classes and walks with a buddy)
- Taking in sunshine and fresh air (hiking, gardening, etc.)
- Organizing and cleaning
- Using renovation exercises, guided mediation, hypnosis and or EFT Tapping to relieve stress
- Keeping a paper notebook for jotting down ideas or asking myself a question
- Acknowledging people I love and appreciate
- Seeking companionship when feeling discouraged
- Coming clean and saying what's so for me with self-love, humor, and personal acknowledgment
- Sharing what I'm up to and what I love about my life

This is my support structure. It covers health, wealth, and community. It gives me focus as I further my career and spiritual growth. While my list is relatively long and specific to me, you'll probably find it includes some elements true for you, too. That being said, I expect you will identify practices and implement supports that uniquely speak to you. That's a beautiful thing.

Feel free to copy and edit anything from my recipes and make it your own. I also invite you to take advantage of the resources, ranging from fun quizzes to workshops, available at www.generating yourownhappiness.com.

Ultimately, we all need support. It usually shows up as seeking advice from authority figures. We look for council and approval of our choices. But, be careful. People tend to give so-called experts more credence than they do themselves and value others' credentials over their own instincts. When you do this, you are disempowering yourself. You may not see it as giving your power away or taking the easy way out, but that's what it is.

Instead of strengthening and gaining support, you weaken your own faculty of discernment.

Let go of beliefs that don't propel you forward. Don't get swept up in short-lived inspiration, especially someone else's inspiration. Know your heart and soul. Inner, purposeful drive produces results—not mimicking someone else's success.

Some think a perfectly manicured, formal topiary garden the height of beauty. I personally prefer the aesthetic of Japanese bonsai, but as you know, growing and caring for bonsai requires a special commitment. I probably have more of the patience required for tending a giant sequoia, the fastest growing conifer on earth. But the point is, what you generate is really a matter of preference and choice. You'll be much happier nurturing and utilizing your natural beauty and strengths versus forcing something that isn't the right fit for you.

People are miserable when trying to be something they're not. They fight to live up to the expectations of others, without questioning if the work is even suited for them. It's like to the proverbial forcing a square peg in a round hole.

Others ask for my support as they aim to accomplish something I've achieved, like finding a companion or building a strong, profitable business. I can outline the steps for them to follow or they could find someone else's recipe for success via the internet, but I don't think that's the best support.

No matter how much someone wants to give you the answer you're looking for, and no matter how much you want to help another person, each individual's soul expansion must come from within. Even though it may not seem like it, you already have access to the knowledge you need.

Here's the catch. Even though you have the answers you're looking for, I believe you are not able to fully grow and expand in solitude. No matter how many hours you spend meditating in silence, you cannot be truly happy without interacting with others. Not only are we hungry for relationships, but other people can also see things that may be in our blind spot.

In my personal experience, when I get stuck and start looking for the "how to", I'm actually wishing for help to get past a hurdle. It may be that I am overwhelmed by the amount of work or insecure about my lack of knowhow and experience. What I need is a trusted friend or counselor to offer perspective. Or perhaps I need to be grounded by practicing a proven physical or spiritual activity. Don't wait until you are stuck to plan who and what you will use for support when the going gets rough.

The modern woman may think the goals she wants to pursue are wealth, prestigious titles, beauty, eternal youth, and a new car, but at our core, every human's true desire is to belong, to feel connected with others, and to be loved. We pride ourselves on being independent, on our ability to pull ourselves up by our own bootstraps, but a sense of social connection is one of our fundamental human needs. This need is never more urgent than when we are creating change or experiencing stress.

We all need companionship and nurturing from time to time. Sometimes all I need is to feel like I have someone on my team. Then, watch out world. Knowing I have support, if needed, makes me feel invincible.

When we experience overwhelm, we tend to procrastinate or work so hard that we fall out of balance and become depleted. When we do this, our relationships suffer. Our bodies suffer. We feel anxious. We lose excitement, motivation, and mojo. We need a proven plan to combat the negative energy and the fear that creeps into our heart.

We all reach a point of overwhelm. For me it often occurs with the thought, *I don't know how.*

Here's an example of how someone else can see your blind spot and help you. I shared with a dear friend and coach of mine that I didn't know how to go about writing a book. I went on to explain that I had never seen myself as a writer. She interrupted before I went too far into my story and said, "I know one thing all writers have in common. They write." It's as Amelia Erhart said, "The most effective way to do it—is to do it." It sounds so simple, but sometimes we need a reminder, a little push, or someone to hold our hand. We need support.

So how do you find the right support for you? That depends. Do you actually have the courage to live the life you dream of? Most people will answer yes to this. However, so often we say we want something, but we don't know how to go about getting it, so how could we be committed to getting it?

To see yourself and the process of change more clearly, get a coach and participate in a strong community. A one-on-one coach won't buy into your story of blame or self-justification. Instead, he or she will ask questions and point you to the answers you're looking for. And I'll tell you again, the answers are within *you*. The guidance you're looking for, your reason for living, and the power to generate your own happiness isn't going to come from an external source. It's got to come from within you. That's the only way.

The real work can be scary. It can be daunting to break out of your comfort zone. You may want to quit. You will second-guess yourself. That's when your coach and a strong community of likeminded people, who are also serious about achieving their dreams, should be by your side. They will support you when you grow weak and face doubt. Ultimately, you must trust yourself and be willing to share your journey with others as you step out to generate your own happiness. Are you ready?

LET'S PLAY:

- IF YOU'RE READY, GO TO WWW.GENERATINGYOUROWNHAPPINESS.COM TO OPTIMIZE YOUR SUPPORT STRUCTURE.

CHAPTER 23

ABOVE ALL, KNOW THYSELF

WHEN SALLY WAS YOUNGER, she was driven by her vision of what future success should look like, and she had lofty goals. The process of acquiring new skills and her eagerness to climb the corporate ladder motivated her to do more. Although she wasn't consciously aware of it, Sally loved learning new things. She thrived on a sense of adventure and a good challenge.

Sally's unhappiness set in when she stopped growing and instead allowed herself to be consumed by a sense of obligation. Without realizing it, she established the habit of self-neglect. She confused service and sacrifice. She stopped directing her focus and let the negativity bias of her mind run the show. It was then that she felt buried under "shoulds" and became stuck in a rut.

You may find yourself stuck in an "in-order-to" mindset or consumed by the search for some grand, predestined purpose. In fact, the search for meaning or significance in life has produced much speculation throughout history. You may experience times when your purpose seems clear and other times when you feel lost. This is all perfectly normal. Just beware that searching for your purpose can be a sexy excuse that keeps you sidetracked. It may consume your energy, causing you to play small instead of being purposeful with what you are given in the moment.

Is it possible that you diddle about, pretending your time is being consumed by urgent matters when, in fact, you are avoiding something? Could it be time to let go of any stories that justify why you're stuck?

If there is a problem, don't waste time identifying the reason why it is the way it is. Rather, trust that every struggle has a purpose. It's not necessary to judge or justify why you are where you are. Remember, the human mind is a meaning-making machine, and your job is to get in touch with your soul. Happiness is not just a string of pleasurable events, it is an inner knowing.

The following practices will contribute to strengthening your ability to generate your own happiness:

- Appreciate everything as it is. Everything and everyone is part of what makes life fascinating and fruitful.
- Question and explore different perspectives.
- Connect with your inner discernment and honor what resonates with you as love and truth.
- Explore your willingness to love, especially your love for humanity.
- Stand at the helm of your life.
- Practice mindfulness, contemplation, and inquiry.
- Act on the gifts you are given.
- Work toward deepening and testing the limits of your full potential.
- Dare to step out of your comfort zone and welcome uncertainty.
- Establish healthy, supportive boundaries.
- Practice letting go of defenses and disempowering beliefs to

dissolve limitations.

- Foster deeply connected relationships and pay it forward by supporting your community.

A valuable "why" to ask yourself may be, "Why do I exist?" Or you could ask, "What do I want?" Do not ask, "Where do I want to be?" There's nowhere to *get to*. And getting "better" at something isn't what you're looking for either. Improving is always comparison based, meaning you have a judgment about yourself in relation to others. Remember, it's the belief that life shouldn't be the way it is that is making you unhappy, not the actual circumstance.

What you focus on grows. I like to think of my future as a canvas, and I can paint anything I like. Most people have the formula for happiness and success backwards. They think happiness will come only after they succeed. By prioritizing your own happiness from the start, all that you say you want is possible.

Real, true success means knowing who you are and what you want. Knowing yourself will ultimately bring freedom. This requires loving, honoring, and trusting your own greatness. Remember, you have a unique expression and gift to share with the world. This gift can change throughout your lifetime as your soul expands and you choose new endeavors, but happiness is always generated by honoring your magnificence and what speaks to your soul. Trust that your quiet voice of intuition simply knows.

Consider that you may already be living the life you designed. If so, it is as perfect as any miracle found in nature and as breathtaking as any work of art. A close friend of mine once compared life to a tree. As a tree grows, it doesn't grow perfectly straight and balanced, even if a horticulturist trains and shapes it. When I think of the events that shape our lives, I can't help but think of the iconic *Jeffrey Pine, Sentinel Dome* photograph by Ansel Adams. Each of our lives is a work of art in progress. No matter our scars, our windblown appearance, we are beautiful.

Remember, you aren't required to change or fix anything about yourself or your life. Even if you feel compelled to completely reinvent yourself, rest assured, you are not broken as is. You may *choose* to create something new from a clean, blank slate or simply make an enhancement here and there, but it's entirely up to you. Release the idea that your life is innately deficient; each person has inherent worth.

If the idea of taking on something new seems daunting, remember, you can lighten the load by letting go of old baggage. If something doesn't resonate with your soul, you don't have to drag it around with you. It may seem like you have no other choice sometimes, but where there's a will, there is a way. You can always give up an old, disempowering story and choose to pursue something new.

You can design your life to maximize generating your own happiness. While you do, think about this: we are drawn by the future, not shaped by the past. Even though you may have derived much of your self-identity from the past, all we really have from the past are stories—and I bet you have some great stories. Joy comes from savoring the moment, and motivation and excitement come from anticipating your future.

LET'S PLAY:

HERE IS MY SIMPLIFIED RECIPE FOR HAPPINESS:

- **COMPASSION FOR ALL BEINGS (INCLUDING ONESELF)**
- **AUTHENTIC SELF-EXPRESSION**
- **TIRELESS DEDICATION TO YOUR PASSION**
- **CURIOSITY**
- **HUMOR**

CHAPTER 24

CALL TO ACTION

IN A WORLD OF great leaders, who have given themselves and their lives for our liberties and for the freedom to pursue happiness, who am I? I am simply someone who has honored the passion and little girl within me. I am someone who can be moved to tears in an instant by thinking of changing the world in a really meaningful way. And I'm really appreciative for my journey and the insight I've gained. But, I would be lying if I didn't confess I still experience fear when putting myself out on the skinny branches and exposing my vulnerabilities. Sometimes, it seems easier to accept a life of mundane existence, but we now know that's not why we're here. This quote from Martin Luther King, Jr. reminds me that achieving any large goal in the face of resistance requires tenacity.

> *"The ultimate measure of a man is not where he stands in*

*moments of comfort and convenience, but where he stands at
times of challenge and controversy."*

When testing the limits of your full potential and taking on a challenge
that is meaningful, you will be faced with resistance. You will experience
setbacks. It takes good old-fashioned grit to keep your goals and persevere.
Research at University of Pennsylvania determined that grit offers better
predictability for ultimate success than IQ. The bottom line is obvious—are
you determined to do whatever it takes to cross the finish line, or are you
looking for glory that comes easily?

I want you to step into your greatness fully. What would be daring for
you to take on for yourself, your life, and the world?

I'm going to be bold and tell you who I think you are. You picked up this
book because there is a strong, beautiful light within you that wants to be
exposed. You are a gift, and the love in your heart wants to be passionately
expressed. You are the next round of leadership, with something amazing
burning inside of you. You have a unique calling and are part of an amazing
group of people who are going to create peace in the world. If I've been
successful with this book, you will go further in your journey toward this
end. This is what I intuitively believe is true about you, and my role is to
support you as you fulfill what you're called to do.

I do have a desired outcome. I want you to be as fully alive and satisfied
as you imagine. I want you to see something for yourself and be inspired
to take action. What's possible for you? You are powerful and capable of
accomplishing anything your heart desires. What are you choosing for your
next chapter? I encourage you to test your own limits. What yearns deep
inside you to be expressed? And what actions are you willing to take to see
it through?

I can't promise you that what you choose to generate will be easy, but I
can promise you that if you give all you've got and honor that which speaks
to you at the soul level, you will not be disappointed.

The demands of daily life may take your attention away from what
you're committed to. You will be faced with obstacles. That's a given. We can
use justification and blame to excuse ourselves from reaching our goals, or

we can direct our focus by eliminating the negative language and checking in with ourselves.

Everything is part of your greater purpose. Arguing with *what is* creates unhappiness. Bringing love to the details of your life generates happiness. Remember, no matter how cliché it sounds, you must love yourself first. You can't love the rest of humanity if you're fighting with yourself. By practicing self-love, you can bring love and curiosity to what it is to be human.

It's time to express yourself fully as the gift you are to the world. It's time to generate your own happiness.

Tag, you're it!

IT'S TIME

IT'S NOW TIME TO GET INTO ACTION,
BUILD STRONG SUPPORT, AND FULLY HONOR
WHAT YOU FEEL CALLED TO DO.
I INVITE YOU TO VISIT
WWW.GENERATEYOUROWNHAPPINESS.COM
AND TAKE ADVANTAGE OF THE
MANY RESOURCES AVAILABLE TO YOU.

FREE DOWNLOAD #1

GO RIGHT NOW TO GET an immediate download of the 100% free checklist, *Ten Things You Could Be Doing to Sabotage Your Happiness.* **www.generatingyourown.com/happiness-sabotage-checklist/.** I've made it easy for you to print this out and use it as a reminder (or maybe as a nudge to change)!

FREE DOWNLOAD #2

WANT ANOTHER TOTALLY FREE gift that can help you get where you want to be faster? You'll love the amazing *10-day Generating Your Own Happiness Challenge.* You'll be surprised at the ease of this! Pick it up here: **www.generatingyourown.com/happiness-10-day-challenge/**

FIND MORE FUN!

I'VE ROLLED UP MY sleeves and opened my heart wide, totally ready to encourage and inspire you, so you'll find an abundance of useful and thought-provoking resources on my website, too. You find them at **www.generatingyourown.com/happiness-resources/**

PLEASE LEAVE A REVIEW

DO YOU KNOW HOW much it helps an author if you leave a review? It makes an amazing difference! I'd be so grateful if you'd write one. All you need to do is enter the book title and then scroll down to where the reviews are left. Super easy! Thank you!

ABOUT THE AUTHOR

IF YOU WANT TO challenge your status quo, soar to new heights, and live a life that fills your heart with joy, meet Cinnamon Alvarez!

She is an entrepreneur who has built four successful businesses. She is an author, speaker, consultant and artist. Her passion for life shows up in all aspects of her work and reputation.

Cinnamon brings business acumen and discernment gained from two decades of growing her successful ceramic lighting manufacturing company in addition to starting an art gallery and operating a group fitness franchise prior to authoring Generating Your Own Happiness: It's Time for Purpose, Passion, and Power.

She has also served as board member and President of the Los Angeles Chapter of NEWH, an international networking and non-profit organization with a mission to raise scholarship funds for deserving students.

She leverages her knowledge and experience as a four-time successful business owner to support others in generating their own happiness in every area of their life. The great honor of contributing to others and seeing them accomplish their wildest dreams feeds her soul.

Made in the USA
Columbia, SC
30 January 2018